Why did Spanish Jewish Convert to Christianity?

HOW IBERIAN JEWS RESPONDED TO PERSECUTION

Juan Marcos Bejarano Gutierrez

Yaron Publishing
Grand Prairie, TX

Copyright © 2019 by Juan Marcos Bejarano Gutierrez.

All rights reserved. No part of this publication may be reproduced, distributed or transmitted in any form or by any means, including photocopying, recording, or other electronic or mechanical methods, without the prior written permission of the publisher, except in the case of brief quotations embodied in critical reviews and certain other noncommercial uses permitted by copyright law. For permission requests, write to the publisher, addressed "Attention: Permissions Coordinator," at the address below.

Juan Marcos Bejarano Gutierrez /Yaron Publishing
701 Forest Park Place
Grand Prairie, Texas 75052
www.CryptoJewishEducation.com

Book Layout ©2017 BookDesignTemplates.com

Ordering Information:
Quantity sales. Special discounts are available on quantity purchases by corporations, associations, and others. For details, contact the "Special Sales Department" at the address above.

Why Did Spanish Jews Convert to Christianity?/ Juan Marcos Bejarano Gutierrez. —1st ed.

Contents

Introduction 6
Jewish Views on Martyrdom 9
The Rhineland Jewish Community 16
    Crypto-Judaism among German Jews 19
Forced Conversion and Early Christians 29
    Conversos and the Jewish Pope 31
The Reasons for Mass Conversions in Spain 33
    The Philosophical Argument 39
Taqiyya and the Jewish Community 44
    The Fatwa of the Mufti of Oran 49
Maimonides' Response to Persecution 59
The Collapse of Faith 71
    The Undermining of Religious Institutions 74
    Christian Influences on Jewish Theology 85
    Shifting Models of Jewish Leadership 88
Conclusions 90
Bibliography 91
Index 103

To my sons Eliel Nathan and Yaron Eliav

"May the angel who hath redeemed me from all evil, bless the lads; and let my name be named in them, and the name of my fathers Abraham and Isaac; and let them grow into a multitude in the midst of the earth."

—GENESIS 48:16

"Thou hast given us like sheep to be eaten; and hast scattered us among the nations."
—Psalm 44:12

Introduction

The mass conversion of Iberian Jews to Christianity in the late 14th and 15th centuries was catastrophic for the Jewish community. Possibly up to a third of the Jewish community converted.[1] There are many reasons why such large-scale conversions occurred. The widespread violence which spread across Castile and Aragon was unprecedented. Violence was the immediate cause for the mass conversions. The debilitated state of Jewish communities following these attacks was also a factor in subsequent waves of conversion.

However, the crisis is also seen as the consequence of an absence of spiritual unity within the Spanish Jewish community. A widespread view is that a rupture developed between ordinary Jews and the wealthy learned Jews serving in royal court positions. The latter is described as unconcerned with Jewish law.[2]

According to this reasoning, some of these individuals were influenced by rationalist philosophy popular within Arabic culture.[3] A class of Jewish courtiers had developed in Andalusia's scholarly atmosphere under Islamic rule during the tenth and eleventh centuries. When the intellectual heirs of this tradition

---

[1] Juan Marcos Bejarano Gutierrez, *Secret Jews: The Complex Identity of Crypto-Jews and Crypto-Judaism* (Grand Prairie: Yaron Publishing, 2016), 38.

[2] Jose Faur, *In the Shadow of History: Jews and Conversos at the Dawn of Modernity* (New York: SUNY, 1992), 1.

[3] Yitzhak Baer, *A History of the Jews in Christian Spain Volume 2* (Philadelphia: Jewish Publication Society, 1961), 253-258.

eventually fell under Christian rule, they progressively quarreled with established Jewish leaders. The latter was ill deposed towards their philosophical tendencies. There were growing circles of mystics known as Kabbalists, whose obscure readings of Jewish texts were, in part, a reaction to the philosophical leanings of those Jews serving the royal court.

The scholar Kevin Ingram has argued that these differing scholarly and mystical tendencies within the Jewish elite unsurprisingly shaped a measure of diffidence in Jewish communities, which was eventually exploited by the Franciscan and Dominican monks. These mendicant orders initiated vigorous evangelizing activities during the fourteenth century. They continued to do so immediately after the catastrophe of 1391.[4] Despite this assault, most of those who relented to the conversion pressure believed that they were not genuinely committing apostasy if they sustained their commitment to Jewish faith clandestinely after their formal initiation into Christianity. Of course, the goal was to eventually return openly to Judaism at the first possible occasion, which did not occur for many. Many Jews were merely pragmatists about the situation they faced. Here Kevin Ingram argues, pragmatism was something that they had absorbed from their leadership.[5]

While the riots in Spain reached an unprecedented level regarding the number of communities affected and the number of Jews targeted, similar attacks occurred in central Europe centuries before. The Jewish community's reactions in the Rhineland in the 11th century to persecution have been compared to the Iberian Jewish community's reactions, often critically connoting the differences in religious fidelity between the two groups. In short, the Jewish settlements of the Rhineland are depicted as much more

---

[4] Kevin Ingram, "Secret lives, public lies: the conversos and socio-religious non-conformism in the Spanish Golden Age." (PhD diss., UC San Diego, 2006), 64.

[5] Ibid., 65.

committed to the Jewish faith because of their supposed willingness to die as martyrs in comparison to their Spanish counterparts.

The accounts of the initial riots in 1391 show that many Spanish Jews did die as martyrs, but the overwhelming majority of Spanish and Portuguese Jews would not. However, the realities regarding the idealized picture of unflagging martyrdom among the Rhineland German communities are much more complicated. They often reveal similarities to the circumstances and decisions their Iberian counterparts would face and make centuries later.

This volume is, in many ways, a continuation of two previous works. The first is *Secret Jews: The Complex Identity of Crypto-Jews and Crypto-Judaism,* and the second *The Rise of the Inquisition: An Introduction to the Spanish and Portuguese Inquisitions.* This first work focused on the Jewish and Christian responses to the mass conversions of Jews in Spain and Portugal. The title focused on the mechanics of one Christian response to Judaizers.

This work focuses on the reasons that many Iberian Jews opted for conversion. The following chapters explore Jewish views on dissimulation and martyrdom and the various influences which may have played a factor in how Iberian Jewish communities responded to persecution and conversion.

CHAPTER 1

Jewish Views on Martyrdom

Dissimulation or the act of concealing one's religious thoughts or ideas has been practiced in varying forms throughout Jewish history. In the Hellenistic period, the mark of circumcision was masked via a painful medical procedure by those Jews who participated in the gymnasium or games. After the fall of the Second Temple, the Romans imposed the *Fiscus Judaicus*, Jewish tax. The historian Suetonius mentions how the Romans were ready to confirm if a man was circumcised, likely indicating that many were hiding their circumcision.

From a Talmudic perspective, if an individual faced the threat of death, all the commandments except murder, incest, and idolatry were allowed to be transgressed. Were the individual presented with the choice of violating these three commandments or death, the individual was expected to choose the latter. The case of extended concealment of the Jewish faith was a complicated issue. The rabbis recognized that observance might be legitimately compromised under coercion or in periods of persecution for extended periods.

In the 5th century CE, practical circumstances applying the Talmud's views were experienced during the Zoroastrian persecution of Jews in Persia. For the most part, the persecution required the neglect of traditional observances instead of the adoption of Zoroastrianism.

The supposed differences in attitude towards martyrdom between Iberian and German Jewish communities in the medieval period may be somewhat exaggerated given the testimony of forced conversions available in German Jewish chronicles and the writings of rabbis like Yehudah HeHasid. The size differences between the two communities are also significant to note when comparing both communities' reactions. However, what is clear is that Ashkenazic communities undoubtedly viewed martyrdom, including self-immolation, as the highest ideal even if it was not always practiced.

Shadrach, Meshach, and Abednego in the Furnace

This almost glorification of martyrdom might be linked to biblical and Talmudic traditions, highlighting approval of martyrdom. Perhaps the most famous is that of Hananiah, Mishael, and

Azariah, i.e., Shadrach, Meshach, and Abednego, in the book of Daniel.[1] The Talmud relates:

> "Why were Hananiah, Mishael, and Azariah willing to give up their lives for the sanctification of the Divine Name? They reasoned comparatively from the frogs [in the account of the second plague]. If in regard to frogs who are not commanded to sanctify the Divine Name, it is written: 'And they shall come up and enter your palace, your bedchamber and your bed, the houses of your courtiers and your people, and your ovens and your kneading bowls...then we who are commanded to sanctify the Divine Name all the more so."[2]

The biblical text's underlying idea and the passage above expresses the view that individuals should be willing to sacrifice their lives to sanctify God's name. Many other examples of Jewish martyrdom can also be found. The *Hasidim*, from I Maccabees, refused to defend themselves on the Sabbath. Another notable case is Hannah and her seven sons. In Second Maccabees, each of the sons, when confronted with death or the choice of life, expresses their commitment to God by reciting a biblical verse. The last son summarizes their views:

> "We have already sworn to the Holy One blessed be he that we shall never exchange him for another god; he likewise swore to us that he will not exchange us for another people."[3]

---

[1] Daniel Chapter 3.

[2] Bavli Pesachim 53b. Robert Chazan, *European Jewry and the First Crusade* (University of California Press: Berkley, 1987), 118.

[3] See Bavli Gittin 57b. Robert Chazan, *European Jewry and the First Crusade* (University of California Press: Berkley, 1987), 119.

While there are many examples of heroic deaths during the Roman period, the qualitative difference lies in capturing or arresting the individuals in question and their execution at the ruling authority's hands. The Talmud provides information on what decision a Jew should take when confronted when the choice of martyrdom or committing murder, idolatry, or sexual immorality.

In these three cases, a Jew is expected to allow himself to be killed rather than transgress. However, it is noteworthy that none other Rabbi Ishmael argued that a Jew faced with such circumstances should choose idolatry over death when presented with this choice in private.[4] However, the majority position was articulated by Rabbi Eliezer, who interpreted the Shema as connoting the idea of martyrdom should it prove necessary in public or private.[5]

Whether Iberian Jewry may have adopted the perspective of Rabbi Ishmael as opposed to the views of Rabbi Eliezer is only speculation. Still, given the Islamic influence on Iberian Jewry, this may not be so outlandish. Nevertheless, the reactions of the Ashkenazic communities in Worms, Mainz, and Cologne, which did not merely include martyrdom but included self-immolation require additional review.

The Talmud does provide some point of reference when it relates to the fate of four hundred youths who opted for self-imposed martyrdom rather than be faced with the likelihood of sexual defilement. The youths asked themselves the following:

> "If we drown in the sea, will we reach the life of the world to come...the senior among them explained: 'The LORD said, I will retrieve from Bashan, I will retrieve from the depths of the sea.' I will retrieve from Bashan' – from out of the teeth of lions; 'I will from the depths of the sea' –

---

[4] Bavli Ketubah 19a; Bavli Sanhedrin 74a.

[5] Robert Chazan, *European Jewry and the First Crusade* (University of California Press: Berkley, 1987), 117.

those who drown in the sea.' When the girls heard this, they all jumped and fell into the sea. The boys reasoned further concerning themselves: 'If this is the response of those for whom such acts are natural, for us, for whom such acts are unnatural, all the more so.' They likewise jumped into the sea. In regard to these youngsters, Scriptures says: 'It is for your sake that we are slain all day long.'"[6]

The idea of self-sacrifice had been accepted as the ideal by Jews in the Rhineland. Those who survived by baptism or even perhaps by fleeing appear to have struggled with the failure to live up to this expectation. An account in *Sefer Hasidim* relates the case of two Jews who submitted to baptism. The story tells that,

"In a certain place many Jews were slain in sanctification of God's name and a few were converted, since they did not allow themselves to be killed and they were baptized...there were two who slaughtered themselves but were not able to put an end to their lives, and the Gentiles thought that they were dead even though they were not. Years later they died, and a certain Jew dreamt that those who were actually slain said to them [in paradise], 'You shall not enter our company since you were not killed in the sanctification of the name as we were.' They proceeded to show that their necks were cut, but the others responded, 'Still, you did not die,' Then an elderly man approached and said: 'Because you wounded yourselves with intention to kill and because you were not

---

[6] Bavli Gittin 57B, Robert Chazan, *European Jewry and the First Crusade* (University of California Press: Berkley, 1987), 123.

baptized in their water, it is appropriate for us to be with you,' and they brought them into their company."[7]

However, while suicide or death was idealized by the Hebrew Chroniclers detailing the Crusades and *Sefer Hasidim* combined a measure of tolerance for those Jews, likely the majority, who had chosen baptism rather than death. Whether they lacked faith or just were not capable of voluntarily submitting to death, *Sefer Hasidim* was willing to offer a measure of understanding by appealing to none other than Abraham. Abraham had failed to admit that Sarah was his wife before Pharaoh and before Abimelech, exposing her to adultery.

> "If Abraham our forefather feared [for Sarah's chastity], why did he go to Egypt? For he was hungry, and he reasoned that if he would not go to Egypt [as in Gen.12] or to Gerar [Gen. 20] all the members of his household might perish from hunger. It was preferable for him to be in doubt as to whether or not they would take Sarah so that they not die of hunger. Now, can a man tell his wife, 'Say that he is my brother,' so that he should not be killed and that they violate her? Did not the sages teach that one must be killed rather than transgress the prohibition of adultery? Rather, Abraham decided to say that she was his sister in order to be saved; and if they would violate her, she, a captive, would be a totally unwilling partner and therefore not forbidden [to Abraham]. Moreover, if he would not say that she was his sister, they would kill him and take her, such that would remain permanently among the uncircumcised, and they would compel her to abandon the rest of the commandments as well. Yet when he said that she was his sister, he could prepare her food and see to it

---

[7] Jeremy Cohen, "Between Martyrdom and Apostasy: Doubts and Self-Definition in Twelfth-Century Ashkenaz," Journal of Medieval and Early Modern Studies 29:3 (1999): 455.

that she would observe the commandments, and additionally, he could pray that [Pharaoh] not touch her."[8]

In summary, the author of *Sefer Hasidim* understood that those unwillingly to commit suicide or offer themselves to be killed could, like Abraham, "temporarily live in sin" for the sake of ensuring their survival as well as that of their families and their future generations. Jeremy Cohen denotes that while the idea of martyrdom existed in Ashkenazic Jewish, the realization that not all could achieve this was also understood. Cohen states:

> "In legal terms, the wish 'to be saved' (le-hinnazel) hardly justified that choice; the rabbinic dictum 'that one must be killed rather than transgress' mandated the opposing decision. Yet *Sefer Hasidim* appears to sympathize, perhaps to condone, and certainly not condemn outright."[9]

Antonio Ciseri's Martyrdom of the Seven Maccabees

---

[8] Jeremy Cohen, "Between Martyrdom and Apostasy: Doubts and Self-Definition in Twelfth-Century Ashkenaz," Journal of Medieval and Early Modern Studies 29:3 (1999): 456.

[9] Ibid., 457.

CHAPTER 2

The Rhineland Jewish Community

For details of the riots in the Rhineland, we are reliant on a few available testimonies. The chronicles detailing attacks on Germany Jewry during the First Crusade also reveal coaxing of Jews by local Christians that led to conversions of the former. As Robert Chazan notes, the conversions could take various forms. Brutal physical force could be applied. In the case of German Jewry, the city of Moers demonstrates a different approach.

> "They killed some of them. Those whom they left alive, they baptized against their will. They did with them as they wished."[1]

In the case of German Jewry, some authorities intervened and forcibly converted Jews in an attempt to assuage the uncontrollable violence of the Crusaders. Consequently, they saved themselves, their subjects, and possibly even the Jews in their vicinity.[2] The second coercive method was the threat of physical force. This

---

[1] Robert Chazan, *European Jewry and the First Crusade* (University of California Press: Berkley, 1987), 101.
[2] Ibid., 101.

could be particularly effective after violence had already claimed the lives of other Jews. This was the case of Jews in Mainz.

PETER THE HERMIT PREACHING THE FIRST CRUSADE.

The third method used in converting Jews was to argue the wisdom of choosing Christianity in light of the destruction and death that had just ensued. One account relating the massacre at Worms records the dialog between the townspeople and a Jewish woman who had survived the onslaught.

> "All of the men of the city gathered and said to her: 'Behold you are a capable woman. Know and see that God does not wish to save you, for they lie naked at the corner of every street, unburied. Sully yourself [with the waters of baptism].' They fell before her to the ground, for they did not wish to kill her. Her reputation was widely known; for all the notables of the city and the princes of the land were found in her circle."[3]

Whether this should be counted as a coerced conversion or as a voluntary conversion is not so simple, I believe. The despair at having seen or known of an oncoming onslaught may have convinced many Jews that resistance was futile being. Robert Chazan

---

[3] Ibid., 102.

argues that no Jewish source verifies the success of such appeals in having Jews convert to Christianity. This may highlight the limited effectiveness of this method or merely reveal Jewish chroniclers' hesitancy to record such events. A Christian account does provide a record of one such occurrence. The Christian authors of *Gesta Trevorum* (Deeds of the Treveri) relate the conversion of a Jewish leader.

> "One of these Jews, a scholar whose name was Micah, said: 'Indeed what you have said is true. It is better that we join the Christian faith than to suffer daily danger to our persons and property.' "[4]

What is perhaps most interesting is a fourth scenario that may reflect many Iberian Jews' perspective. A Jewish chronicle highlighting the attacks on the community at Worms relates the following:

> "There were those of them who said: 'Let us do their will for the time being, and let us go and bury our brethren and save our children from them.' For they had seized the children that remained, 'a small number,' saying that perhaps they would remain in their pseudo-faith. They [the Jews who converted] did not desert their Creator, nor did their hearts incline after the Crucified. Rather they cleaved to the God on high. Moreover, the rest of the community, those who remained the chambers of the bishop, sent garments with which to clothe those who have been killed through those who had been saved, for they were charitable."[5]

Even those converting in the face of these circumstances could undoubtedly feel remorse. A narrative from the period documents

---

[4] Ibid., 102.
[5] Ibid., 103.

the case of Isaac ben David, who quickly regretted his decision to convert.

> "He thought: 'I shall do penitence and be faithful and perfect with the LORD GOD of Israel, to the point where I commend to him, my soul. In his hand, shall I fall. Perhaps, he will do according to His loving-kindness, and I shall still join my comrades and come with them to their circle, to the great light. It is revealed and known before the examiner of the heart that I did not accede to the enemy except in order to save my children from the hands of the wicked and so that they not remain in their pseudo-faith. For they are young and cannot distinguish between good and evil."[6]

Crypto-Judaism among German Jews

In 1096, the communities of Worms, Mainz, and Cologne were the targets of violence by Crusaders traveling to the Holy Land.[7]

---

[6] Ibid., 103-104.

[7] Salo W. Baron, *A Social and Religious History of the Jews Volume IV* (Philadelphia: Jewish Publication Society, 1957), 94-106.

Massacre of the Jews of Metz during the First Crusade

The wholesale persecution against these communities is most often recorded as being death rather than conversion. Three Hebrew chronicles and various *piyyutim* (liturgical poems) describe those Jews who opted for martyrdom.

> "Refusing to compromise their faith and relinquish the fear of our king…they extended their necks for slaughter and offered up their pure souls to their fathers in heaven…Each first sacrificed the other and then, in turn, yielded to be sacrificed, until the streams of blood touched and mingled, and the blood of husbands joined with that of their wives, the blood of fathers and their sons, the blood of brothers and their sisters, the blood of teachers and their pupils, the blood of bridegrooms and their brides…the blood babies and sucklings and their mothers. They were killed and slaughtered for the unity of God's holy and awesome name…Happy are they, and happy is

their lot; for all of them are destined for eternal life in the world to come."[8]

There were other options available, however. As Jeremy Cohen notes, some attempted to evade the marauding Crusaders, while others attempted to bribe them. Others sought asylum with local rulers; some fled the area; some took up arms to fight the Crusaders. In the end, however, the majority of those who survived did so by submitting to baptism.[9] Those converted under duress often continued to practice Judaism to the best of their ability, providing evidence of crypto-Judaism among German Jewry. According to Robert Chazan, the conversions were insincere and typically short-lived. A Jewish chronicle of the period provides details regarding the nature of the crypto-Jewish practices maintained by these converts.

> "Now it is fitting to tell the praise of those forcibly converted. For all that, they ate and drank, they mortally endangered themselves. They slaughtered meat and removed from it the fat. They examined the meat according to the regulations of the sages. They did not drink the wine of libation. They did not go to church except occasionally. Every time they went, they went out of great duress and fear. They went reluctantly. The Gentiles themselves knew that they had not converted wholeheartedly, but only out of fear of the crusaders and that they did not believe in their deity, but that rather they clung to the fear of the LORD and held fast to the sublime God, creator of heaven and earth. In the sight of the Gentiles, they observed the Torah of the LORD secretly. Anyone who

---

[8] Jeremy Cohen, "Between Martyrdom and Apostasy: Doubts and Self-Definition in Twelfth-Century Ashkenaz," Journal of Medieval and Early Modern Studies 29:3 (1999): 434.

[9] Ibid., 434.

speaks ill of them insults the countenance of the Divine Presence."[10]

Despite the existence of crypto-Judaism among German Jewry and the documented conversion of Jews by several sources, there is an assumption that a significant religious distinction between the Jews of Germany and the Iberian Peninsula communities existed. It is also important to note that the scope of the destruction typically assumed to have transpired in German Jewish communities at the Crusaders' hands has been overstated. As Robert Chazan states:

> "As we have seen, the bulk of Ashkenazic Jewry survived the dangerous summer months unscathed; it is therefore not surprising that these events had relatively little impact on the majority of the new Ashkenazic communities."[11]

Many German Jews were not merely willing to undergo death to avoid conversion to Christianity; they were, according to several chroniclers, willing to kill their own families. Albert of Aix provides one such example.

> "The Jews, seeing that their Christian enemies were attacking them and their children, and were sparing no age, fell upon one another-brothers, children, wives, mothers, and sisters-and slaughtered one another. Horrible to say, mothers, cut the throats of nursing with knives and stabbed others, preferring them to perish thus by their own hands rather than be killed by the weapons of the uncircumcised."[12]

Jews even threw themselves into the Rhine River, as in the case of the town of Wevelinghofen.

---

[10] Robert Chazan, *European Jewry and the First Crusade* (University of California Press: Berkley, 1987), 101.
[11] Ibid., 137.
[12] Ibid., 106.

> "When the enemy came before the town, then some of the pious ones ascended the tower and threw themselves into the Rhine River that flows around the two and drowned themselves in the river and died."[13]

There are plenty of other examples of similar events occurring. However, the critical question that must be answered is why German Jews appear to have embraced such a radical step to avoid conversion. In perhaps the most horrifying depiction of Jews opting for death rather than risk the possibility of conversion, we learn that a rabbi was willing to kill even infants over this concern.

> "There is a report of a certain rabbi who slaughtered many infants during a period of forced conversion because he feared that they [the gentiles] would convert them. There was another rabbi with him, who was exceedingly angry with him and called him a murderer. But he [the first rabbi did not waver. The [second] rabbi said: 'If I am correct, let that rabbi be killed in an unusual way.' Thus it was…Subsequently, the persecution subsided. If he had not slaughtered those infants, they would have been saved."[14]

The story of Rabbi Kalonymos ben Meshulam the Pious of Mainz is often pointed to as an example of the circumstances faced by Jews in the Rhineland.

---

[13] Ibid., 109.
[14] Ibid., 157.

Strasbourg Pogrom 1349

However, the story reveals a variety of broader issues. It serves to understand the circumstances Jews in Castile and Aragon also faced as well. As a parnas (warden) of the Jewish community of Mainz, Rabbi Kalonymos tried to contact King Henry IV in the wake of the continuing Crusader onslaught. When this failed, he attempted to raise arms against them. In the end, amid the slaughter of approximately 1000 Jews in Mainz, Rabbi Kalonymos and fifty-three others took refuge in a local bishop's chambers. From there, the story tells us that,

> "They entered into the vestry [*meltahah*] in the church [*ba-avodah zarah*], a storage room which is called the sacristy. They remained there in oppressive conditions [*be-zar uve-mazoq*] because of the threatening sword. The door of the vestry was narrow, and it was dark so that none of the enemy noticed them, and they were utterly silent [va-yehi ke-maharish]. The sun had set, and there was thick darkness; they cried out in distress, and their tongues clung to their palates [*ve-davaq leshonam el hikkam*] from thirst. They approached the window and spoke to the sacristan, requesting that he give them water so as to revive themselves, but he refused. They finally gave him ten

silver coins for a flask full of water, to fulfill the biblical verse, 'You shall serve your enemies [...] in hunger and thirst,' etc. He brought the flask to the window but was unable to hand it to them because the opening was too narrow. Finally, he brought a lead pipe through which he passed the water, and they drank moderately, but did not quench their thirst..."[15]

A messenger for the bishop had assured Rabbi Kalonymos of the former's pledge to protect them. This pledge had been given only after Rabbi Kalonymos had requested the bishop to swear. In the end, the bishop defaulted on his word or was unable to provide the protection he had intended. The account relates the bishop's subsequent harsh statement to the besieged Jews.

"I cannot save you, and your God has turned away from you and does not wish to allow any of your group to survive. From now on, it is no longer in my power to save or help you. Know now what you and your associates must do: Either believe in our faith or pay for the iniquity of your forefathers."[16]

In the end, Rabbi Kalonymos and those with him agreed to opt for suicide rather than embrace Christianity. According to the account, in unison, they recited the "blessing over their self-sacrifice ['*aqedatam*]."

Jeremy Cohen analyzes Rabbi Kalonymos and his followers' flight further in a manner that may reveal a subtle critique of those Jews who had submitted to baptism as a means of saving their lives. He states

---

[15] Jeremy Cohen, "Between Martyrdom and Apostasy: Doubts and Self-Definition in Twelfth-Century Ashkenaz," Journal of Medieval and Early Modern Studies 29:3 (1999): 436-437.

[16] Ibid., 437.

"...the refuge which they sought, the residence and sacristy of the bishop, proves to be no viable refuge at all. There Kalyonymos and his group find the conditions most oppressive; they are uncomfortable; they thirst for water, and what is provided proves inadequate and unsatisfying; their guardians deceive them. These fifty-four Jews have sought to escape death and preserve life in a state of veritable limbo; shrouded in thick darkness, they find neither the light of day nor the light of paradise enjoyed by the martyrs as an immediate consequence of their deaths. There, in the church (literally,' in the idolatrous worship,' ba-avodah zarah), they lose their identity; they can neither see nor be seen; we read that 'they cried out in distress' but yet that 'they were utterly silent.'" [17]

The Hebrew terms used in the narrative reveal intentional allusions to idolatry in the Hebrew Bible. The word *meltahah*, Cohen notes, appears only once in the *Tanach* in 2 Kings,10:22, where it refers to Baal's worshippers' distinctive clothing.

---

[17] Ibid., 437. Cohen also finds connection to Jeremiah 19:4-9 which echoes the prophecy of Deuteronomy and which Cohen argues could have easily been applicable to those Jews who had not martyred themselves but instead submitted to baptism. "For they have forsaken me...to put their children to the fire as burnt offerings to Baal- which I never commanded, never decreed, and which never came to my mind...I will cause them to fall by the sword before their enemies...and I will cause them to eat the flesh of their sons and the flesh of their daughters, and they shall devour one another's flesh-because of the desperate straits [be-zar uve-mazoq] to which they will be reduced by their enemies, who seek their life [*nafasham*]. Jeremy Cohen, "Between Martyrdom and Apostasy: Doubts and Self-Definition in Twelfth-Century Ashkenaz," Journal of Medieval and Early Modern Studies 29:3 (1999): 439-440.

Plundering the Jewish ghetto in Frankfurt am Main August 1614

The story in question is that of King Jehu, who acted subversively to punish Israelites who had "donned" idolaters' clothing. Also, the phrase *be-zar uvemazoq* is found in various biblical passages, including Deuteronomy 28:53-57, which states,

> "You shall eat your own issue, the flesh of your sons and daughters that the LORD your God has given you, because of the desperate straits [*bemazor uve-mazoq*] to which your enemy shall reduce you."[18]

What elements provided German Jewry with sufficient confidence to adopt such seemingly extreme actions? While the example above shows that some rabbis objected to such actions, Jewish and Christian chronicles corroborate the chosen self-sacrifice option. The justification for these actions is rooted in part in the Talmudic tradition, though alternative perspectives can be found.

---

[18] Ibid., 437.

CHAPTER 3

Forced Conversion and Early Christians

Turning back to Spain's situation, oddly enough, early Christianity's critical players may have provided forced converts in Spain with some measure of hope after their conversion experiences. At least the legends that were circulating among Jews at the time. Christians often assume Jews simply rejected the New Testament. Instead, alternative folktales regarding key New Testament persons were often disseminated in the Jewish community. To what extent such stories circulated among Jews are unclear, but they were sufficiently spread for Christian authorities to be aware of them. Early Christian characters' alternative stories may provide the most amazing positive examples of subversion, self-sacrifice, and divine purpose.

Jewish tradition first rooted in the polemical work of *Toldot Yeshu* (The Story of Jesus) saw individuals such as Peter and Paul, the early proponents of Christianity, as having lived double lives. On the surface, these individuals had abandoned Judaism. While based on Jewish ideas, they had founded a movement that had quickly veered from its Jewish origins. Their purpose in sacrificing their identity was purportedly to ensure that the new movement was sufficiently distinct from Judaism and ensure the Jewish people's welfare and continued existence. Simon Peter was Rabbi Simon Kaipha, who had only feigned conversion to Christianity to rise to its leadership. As a leader, he replicated the miracles of Jesus. He used his power to ensure that a clear separation between Judaism and Christianity would arise since, in its early days, the distinctions were not so clear. Also, he converted and gained reigns of the movement to make sure that Christians would not murder Jews. According to one source, another principal objective of the dissimulating Peter was to guarantee that forced conversions would not be enacted.

> "From now on, you shall not force [one] to adopt your faith and be coerced to undergo baptism, unless he does so voluntarily. If you would force the Jews to convert to your religion, they might understand that your religion is not good. Thus, each one who converts should do so by his free will. And even if he says that he comes of his own will, he will only be accepted after he has sat for thirty days in the home of good people; and any child younger than nine years of age you shall not receive since he cannot understand what it is he does."[1]

The scholar Ram Ben-Shalom notes that Simon Peter appears to be the first figure in Jewish sources portrayed as a false convert. His actions embody the idea of *mitzvah habah b'averah,* the view that a commandment can be fulfilled through a transgression. According to these sources, while Simon Peter acted as a pope of Christianity, he clandestinely maintained his links to the Jewish community. He even authored several liturgical poems that are part of the synagogue liturgy. These liturgical pieces include the *Nishmat Kol Chai*, the *Eten Tehilah* (one of the liturgical poems of Yom Kippur), and other Piyyutim (liturgical poems such as the *Berachot haSheer*).[2] In what appears to be a counter-story to a

---

[1] A. Jellinek, *Beit Ha-Midrash, Vol. 6.* (Jerusalem: Bamberger et Vahrman, 1938), 10.

[2] Jakob Jocz, *The Jewish People and Jesus Christ* (Grand Rapids: Baker Book House, 1949), 201, 383. See also Joseph

passage in Romans in which Paul declares his willingness to lose his own soul 'that Israel might be saved,' one version of the Toldot Yeshu states

> "It is preferable to lose Shimon and one hundred others like him than to lose one Jewish soul."[3]

Conversos and the Jewish Pope

The most striking example of a covert emissary is the story of a Jewish pope that perhaps more than Peter or Paul's examples appear much more connected to forced converts' experience. The story appears likely based on the actual case of Pope Anacletus II (1130-1138), whose parents were Jewish converts to Christianity. Despite their conversion and studies, accusations were levied against him that he stole from the Church and distributed holy vessels to Jews.[4] According to the story, a child named Elchanan was kidnapped by a Christian servant. Elchanan was the son of Rabbi Simon, the Great of Mainz.

The story relates that nuns raised Elchanan, and grew up to become a great scholar until he was elected as Pope. Despite his rearing, Elchanan was conscious of his Jewish background and believed he was fulfilling some Divine mission. Unbeknownst to him, the mission was to protect Jews from Christian oppression. Elchanan surrounded himself with Jewish advisors, and his beneficence towards Jews was unequaled. Like many Conversos, Elchanan remained Christian because of his prominent position

---

Klausner, *Jesus of Nazareth* (New York: The Macmillan Company, 1943), 50-51.
   [3] A. Jellinek, *Beit Ha-Midrash, Vol. 6.* (Jerusalem: Bamberger et Vahrman, 1938), 9.
   [4] A. Jellinek, *Beit Ha-Midrash, Vol. 5.* (Jerusalem: Bamberger et Vahrman, 1938), xxxviii.

and his property. When, according to the story, Elchanan met his father, he asked the following:

> "Father, can you tell me if there is hope for me after this life? Will God have mercy on me? Rabbi Shimon answered: 'My dear son! Purge this concern from your heart for you were a forced convert [anus], and while still a boy you were taken from your father and your faith.' 'But father!' his son continued, 'I have long known that I was born a Jew and in spite of this, I have continued to live among the Gentiles to this very day. The comforts I had were what kept me from returning to the true God. Will God forgive me?' Simon answered: 'Nothing stands in the way of repentance [teshuba].'"[5]

There are various alternate endings to the story. One version has Elchanan returning to Mainz and living openly as a Jew. Before doing so, he writes a polemical work undermining Christianity and orders that all successors to the papacy read this work. Another version ends with Elchanan committing an act of suicide right after declaring his rejection of Christianity.[6]

---

[5] Ibid., 151.

[6] Ram Ben-Shalom, "The Converso as Subversive: Jewish Traditions or Christian Libel?" Journal of Jewish Studies 50:2 (1999): 259-283.

CHAPTER 4

The Reasons for Mass Conversions in Spain

The motivations for the large-scale conversions of 1391 in Castile and Aragon were directly connected to the violent attacks that Jewish communities across the Peninsula endured. For some individual Jews, however, the option of conversion may not have been that problematic as embracing Christianity could indeed prove beneficial in various ways. In 1385, for example, Isaac Xam and his son Vidal faced a severe economic crisis linked to a massive debt they had incurred. Imprisoned, Isaac and Vidal appealed to King Pere (Peter) I of Aragon with the following proposal. They offered to convert in exchange for royal protection. On November 2, 1385, the king responded positively by granting them remission and protection over their property claims. Another named Pere Desplà also appealed to the King regarding his financial situation. Imprisoned as surety for his debts, he proposed to travel to Majorca to convert his family. The king granted him six-month probation during which he was to journey to the island and carry out his mission.[1] The extent to which financial

---

[1] Alexandra Guerson, "Seeking Remission: Jewish Conversion in the Crown of Aragon, c. 1378-1391," Jewish History Volume 24 Issue 1 (2010): 36.

circumstances could lead someone to convert is argued by Alexandra Guerson, who writes:

> "The higher demand for taxes led to increased tensions within Jewish communities. Jewish quibbled over the proper distribution of taxes within their aljamas, but they also paid close attention to those who attempted to evade taxes or had acquired exemptions from contributing. In this climate, marginal Jews, whose precariousness was only worsened by economic crisis and over-taxation, may easily have considered conversion, for at least they would thereby be able to place food on the table. Excessive taxation in thirteenth-century England...generated enmity, if not a full break down of relationships within Jewish communities."[2]

Peter I receiving a shield emblazoned with St George's Cross.

---

[2] Ibid., 40.

Facing economic challenges, an orphan, a widow, and others viewed as unsustainable burdens on the families may have viewed conversion as the only realistic option.[3] The Crown's willingness to assist those who converted must have indeed painted an attractive option. In 1382, King Pere extended a Conversa named Caterina and her children special protection. She was granted safe conduct and allowed to receive alms. Her husband was held captive in North Africa, whose fate must have been uncertain at best. That same year, King Pere granted another Jewish woman who converted to Christianity the right to collect alms and receive offerings anywhere in his domains.[4] Whatever mean existed in the Jewish community to support such families was either insufficient or had broken down.

Conflicts with family members could also prove to be a rationale for conversion. In 1383, one family in the town of Xativa in Aragon threatened to convert if they were punished with excommunication or prison for offenses they had committed. In 1375, another Aragonese family appealed to the rabbinic court to not excommunicate their family member. The man in question had taken a concubine in defiance of a promise he had made to his wife. If excommunicated for his offense, the family was convinced he would convert to Christianity.[5]

In the Kingdom of Castile, Rabbi Yom Tov Ishbili related that a man had threatened to convert to Christianity if the rabbis prohibited him from marrying the woman he chose.[6] Escaping corporal punishment was also a benefit that conversion to Christianity could achieve. In 1381, Jaume Romeu was sentenced to lashes as punishment for an unspecified crime. He appealed to

---

[3] Ibid., 40.
[4] Ibid., 37.
[5] Ibid., 39.
[6] Ibid., 41.

the king, who pardoned him after he and his wife and five children converted to Christianity.[7]

Depiction of Don Isaac Abarbanel

Before reviewing the more profound and more widespread reasons behind the mass conversions, Don Isaac Abarbanel provides a review of some immediate ones.

> "Because of the miseries, the condemnations, and the massacres by the enemies, they left the totality of the Law, and they thought to become like one of the people of the land."[8]

Fear of expulsion or violence also loomed in the background for many and indeed formed a basis for many converting. Even those

---

[7] Alexandra Guerson, "Seeking Remission: Jewish Conversion in the Crown of Aragon, c. 1378-1391," Jewish History Volume 24 Issue 1 (2010): 37.

[8] Jose Faur, "Four Classes of Conversos: A Typological Study," Revue des Etudes Juives, CXLIX (1-3), Janiver-Juin (1990): 113-124.

Conversos who had converted out of sincerity, such as Abner of Burgos in the 14th century, admitted that the status of Jewish life had revealed to him the hopelessness of the Jewish dilemma. Burgos stated:

> "I saw the poverty of the Jews, my people, from whom I am descended, who have been oppressed and broken and heavily burdened by taxes throughout their long captivity – this people that has lost its former honor... and there is none to help or sustain them... when I had meditated on the matter, I went to the synagogue weeping sorely and sad at heart. And I prayed... And in a dream, I saw the figure of a tall man who said to me, 'Why dost thou slumber? Hearken unto these words...for I say unto thee that the Jews have remained so long in captivity for their folly and wickedness and because they have no teacher of righteousness through whom they may recognize the truth.'"[9]

Regarding the forced relocation of Jews from some regions of the cities to more segregated areas, Solomon Alami, in *Iggeret ha-musar* wrote in 1415,

> "We have been banished from our homes to the field and to the dung-gate..."[10]

The financial assistance they may have received for those suffering from poverty due to converting was often sufficient. For example, it was customary for the authorities of Cervera to give a monetary gift to each Jews who became a Christian. This is reflected in a document dated 1424 that relates that the *paers* or magistrates of the community had given the year before, a "cota de un valor de 23 sueldos" to a Jew who had been baptized. It was

---

[9] Yitzhak Baer, *A History of the Jews in Christian Spain Volume 1* (Philadelphia: Jewish Publication Society, 1961), 328-329.
[10] Ibid., 241.

customary, the document notes to donate something for the love of God.[11]

While these were primary reasons, scholars understand why Spanish Jews converted in such large numbers in contrast to other Jewish communities faced with desperate circumstances. Yosef Hayim Yerushalmi notes the following:

> "Will we ever know how many Jews were lost over the years? Amongst the Jews who were lost must be counted not only those who were the victims of massacres and martyrdoms but equally those who went over to the other side or converted. And these Jews were lost not because- as the most simplistic explanation would have it- they were seduced by purely secular ambitions or material benefits; they were conquered by real, genuine despair; they feared that the Jewish people had no future."[12]

Abner of Burgos and other sincere apostates were often the bitterest representatives of anti-Jewish sentiment. They actively worked to erode the viability of the Jewish community. In a seeming obsession to prove the weakness and futility of Jewish faith, Burgos helped instigate the intensified harassment of the Jews by devising a hypothesis that included the requirement and validation of such maltreatment. He argued that the elimination of Jewish "self-rule" prevented Jewish realization of the Messiah's true identity. The Messiah would not be revealed to Jews,

> "...until the Jews possess no authority, not even such petty authority as is exercised over them by their rabbis

---

[11] Josep M. Llobet Portella, "Los conversos Segun La documentacion local de Cervera (1338 -1501)," Revista de la Fac-ultad de Geografia e Historia, num 4, (1989): 337.

[12] Yerushalmi quoted in Brbau, Pierre, "Exile, Assimilation, and Identity: from Moses to Joseph," in Carlebach, et al. 250. Shelomo Alfassa, *The Sephardic 'Anousim': Anousim, Crypto-Jews, and Marranos* (New York, Alfassa: 2010), 48-49.

and communal wardens, those coarse creatures who lord it over the people like kings. They hold out vain promises to them in order to keep them under constant control. Only with the elimination of these dignitaries and judges and officers will salvation come to the masses."[13]

Abner was obsessed that he did not exhibit fear in casting blame on either the Pope or the Christian monarchs he believed had failed to subjugate the Jews sufficiently. Jews would only experience salvation,

"When many Jewish communities are massacred, and the particular generation of Jews is thereby reduced in numbers, some Jews immediately convert to the dominant Christian faith out of fear, and in that way, a handful are saved… and the pain of impoverishment will lead to an increase of shamelessness among them; that is, they will no longer be ashamed to profess the truth openly and convert to Christianity."[14]

Subsequent converts adopted Abner's approach like Pablo de Santa Maria and Geronimo de Santa Fe.

The Philosophical Argument

The violence notwithstanding, many believe that other reasons predisposed so many Iberian Jews to opt for conversion. A primary assumption is that the rise of Maimonidean and the philosophical tradition brought about the tendency of many Jews to opt for conversion in the face of persecution (physical, economic, or cultural). This view is based on the idea that secular knowledge and philosophical studies created skepticism towards Judaism by

---

[13] Yitzhak Baer, *A History of the Jews in Christian Spain Volume 1* (Philadelphia: Jewish Publication Society, 1961), 350.
[14] Ibid., 353-354.

those following it. Jose Faur sums up the issue succinctly when he states:

> "When studying the large numbers of Jews converting to Christianity in Spain and Portugal, scholars are quick to point out to the Maimonidean tradition-the cultural and philosophical heritage developed in Jewish Andalusia- as a principal factor in the collapse of Jewish life. The general premise is that secular knowledge and sophistication foster defection from Judaism. This judgment itself and the basic suppositions it comprises are the product of one of the most profound religious controversies during the Jewish Middle Ages: whether to accept the religious notions of Christian society as the perimeter of Jewish spiritual life."[15]

The eminent historian Yitzhak Baer, in his work *History of the Jews in Christian Spain,* also summarizes the typical view:

> "There were many, it would seem, in Spain, who found in Maimonidean philosophy convenient support for their extreme liberalism...These men accepted only a faith of reason and rejected popular beliefs. They put rational understanding ahead of the observance of the commandments... [and] denied the value of Talmudic Aggadot."[16]

Several Jewish sources of the period support this view. Baer finds some support in the 15th-century writings of Solomon Alami, Shem Tov ben Shem Tov, Isaac Arama, and Joel ibn Shuaib.

This view is also embraced by Cecil Roth, who states:

---

[15] Jose Faur, *In the Shadow of History: Jews and Conversos at the Dawn of Modernity* (New York: SUNY, 1992), 1.

[16] Yitzhak Baer, *A History of the Jews in Christian Spain* Volume 1 (Philadelphia: Jewish Publication Society, 1961), 97.

"Their immemorial residence in the country made them think of themselves solely as Iberians: their philosophical interests and rationalizing tendencies had minimized the cleavage between the various faiths: their intimate social and business relations with their fellow-countrymen made the step of conversion seem less drastic: and to many of these cultured men of affairs free enjoyment of their goods and chattels appeared to be well worth an occasional mass."[17]

Alami, for example, held that the philosophical movement was the primary cause of Jewish collapse. Alami argued that the elevation of philosophy, intellect, systematic search and natural inquiry undermine obedience to the commandments.[18] Shem Tob continued the critique of philosophy as a cause of Jewish communal life but targeted Aristotelian thought specifically, which promoted the idea of an impersonal God.

For Shem Tob, a God removed from the human activity sphere undermined Jewish convictions that God would ultimately judge people with appropriate reward and punishment. Shem Tov ben Shem Tov believed that an impersonal God's belief and eliminating belief in an afterlife inevitably diminished fidelity to Judaism.[19] Shem Tov's possible contribution to the decline of Jewish life is a subject we will address shortly. Rabbi Isaac Arama blamed philosophically oriented individuals for compromising the Torah since they believed that

---

[17] Cecil Roth, *the Spanish Inquisition* (New York: W.W. Norton and Company, 1964), 24.

[18] Allan Harris Cutler and Helen Elmquist Cutler, *The Jews as Ally of the Muslim: Medieval Roots of Anti-Semitism* (Notre Dame: University of Notre Dame, 1986), 273.

[19] Ibid., 274.

"...what is written in the Scriptures and all that is implied there, is not literally true but is rather an allegory meant for the masses of men, who are unable to comprehend the truths of philosophy; but only that which conforms to philosophy, whether in its literal sense or in the light of either temperate or intemperate interpretations, is to be regarded as true. And this belief of theirs seems to me to be truly remarkable, for if it is indeed correct, then the holy Torah would serve no purpose at all, and Israel would undoubtedly have been better off without it, whether interpreted literally or any other way."[20]

According to this dominant view, the cause is that the philosophical leanings reflected in pro-Maimonidean circles resulted in the spread of Averroism, a school of metaphysics that rose by the stimulus of the 12th century Andalusian Muslim philosopher Averroës. Averroës worked on reconciling Aristotelianism with Islam. This approach would be followed by several Christian philosophers and by Maimonides.[21] Joel ibn Shuaib argued that Jews lost belief in the coming of Messiah. Without explaining why ibn Shuaib contended that Iberian Jews had abandoned the messianic hope and consequently rendered hopes of any future redemption mute.

According to the scholar Gerson Cohen, rationalism helped undermine faith creating doubt about miracles such as the

---

[20] Yitzhak Baer, *A History of the Jews in Christian Spain*, Volume 2 (Philadelphia: Jewish Publication Society, 1961), 257.

[21] Jose Faur, *In the Shadow of History: Jews and Conversos at the Dawn of Modernity* (New York: SUNY, 1992), 235. See also Jose Faur, *Anti-Maimonidean Demons,* Netanya College and Jose Faur, *A Crisis of Categories: Kabbalah and the Rise of Apostasy in Spain*, Bar Ilan University and Norman Roth, *Conversos, Inquisition, and the Expulsion of the Jews from Spain* (Madison: University of Wisconsin, 1995), 11.

resurrection, which discouraged martyrdom.²² I believe three issues must be taken into consideration in reviewing the Converso dilemma. The first is a subject that does not appear to be noted in most discussions on the issue. This is the influence of the Islamic concept of *Taqiyya* and its role in how Iberian Jewish communities may have understood conversion as a viable option. The second is the changing nature and decline of Spanish rabbinic scholarship and the anti-Maimonidean controversy whose effects on Spanish Jewish society are largely ignored. Tied to this, is the rise of Kabbalah and various views of reincarnation introduced along with it. The last issue is Maimonides' views on dissimulation, arguably reflected in his letter, *Iggeret Hashamad*.

---

²² Mark R. Cohen, *Under Crescent and Cross: The Jews in the Middle Ages* (Princeton: Princeton University Press, 1994), 175.

CHAPTER 5

Taqiyya and the Jewish Community

The Islam conquest of the Iberian Peninsula began in 711 CE and extended over parts of the peninsula through the end of the 15th century until King Ferdinand's and Queen Isabella's victory over the Kingdom of Granada. While the *Reconquista* increasingly carved out large sections of Spanish soil formerly under Islamic rule, the influence of Islamic culture on Jewish communities, especially in the area of religion, remained strong through the 13th and 14th centuries. Persecution was understood differently by Jews in Islamic lands or previously under Islamic rule. Menahem Ben-Sasson notes that under Islamic rule, Jews underwent extensive cultural Arabization.[1] The influence of Islamic-Arabic culture in the area of religious thought is also evident. Major Jewish religious works were produced in Arabic. The philosophical trend present in Arabic thought bled over into Jewish thinking most pronounced in Maimonides' philosophical works. Consequently, responses to a whole host of issues, including persecution, were understood differently by Jews in Islamic domains. These

---

[1] Menahem Ben-Sasson, "On the Jewish Identity of Forced Converts: A Study of Forced Conversion in the Almohade Period." Pe'amim 42 (1990): 20.

concepts likely remained in force even after the demise of Islamic domination.

In Christian Europe, as we have seen, martyrdom or suicide was mostly the preferred response to forced conversions. Whether this attitude toward martyrdom was, as Mark Cohen asserts, an elaboration of the martyr traditions recorded in the *Midrash* is unclear.[2] Jacob Katz argues that Ashkenazi views of martyrdom were also influenced by their conviction that Christianity was idolatrous. However, no Sephardic source to my knowledge considered Christianity to be otherwise. Their views were further influenced by the willingness of Christians to suffer martyrdom. If Christians were willing to suffer martyrdom, so should Jews. There were indeed examples of martyrdom and even self-immolation among Iberian Jews. However, the numbers percentage-wise were smaller if only because of the disparities in the population. In Gerona, we learn that

> "...the Jews claimed that the number of the dead was larger, but the *jurados* pointed out that many Jews-women and children- had been slain by the Jews themselves. The honorable city fathers were unwilling to debit their account with the lives of those holy innocents who committed suicide in order to escape forced conversion."[3]

Mark Cohen also notes that conversion to escape death likely occurred to a higher degree than alluded to in Hebrew accounts of the period, but martyrdom remained the Ashkenazi ideal.[4] Nevertheless, Rabbi Yehudah HeChasid's references to both apostates and various acts of dissimulation in his *Sefer Chasidim* make it clear that the situation was more complicated in Ashkenazic

---

[2] Mark R. Cohen, *Under Crescent and Cross: The Jews in the Middle Ages* (Princeton: Princeton University Press, 1994), 174.

[3] Yitzhak Baer, *A History of the Jews in Christian Spain, Volume 2* (Philadelphia; Jewish Publication Society, 1961), 107.

[4] Ibid., 175.

lands than is often appreciated.⁵ Rabbi Yehudah, for example, points to an example in Rokeach 316 and Teshuvot Maharil 118.

> "When the members of his community were offered the alternative of either converting or being killed, he [the rabbi] advised them to convert and afterward to return to Judaism…when things settled down, they all returned to Judaism. Nevertheless, since the rabbi counseled his flock to defect from the Jewish faith, his offspring all became apostates, and he is being punished [in the hereafter] as though he was the one who had caused them to sin."⁶

It is important to note that Jews did not maintain the same invectives against Islam that Ashkenazi Jews maintained toward Christianity. More importantly, the concept of martyrdom was not a similarly significant concept in Islam as it was in Christianity. As Cohen notes, in Islam, the martyr is a warrior who dies fighting in a holy war. Suicide or execution to evade conversion is not held in the same light.

The Sunni Islamic scholar Abdul Hamid Siddiqui defines *Taqiyya* as,

> "Concealing or disguising one's beliefs, convictions, ideas, feelings, opinions, and/or strategies at a time of imminent danger, whether now or later in time, to save oneself from physical and/or mental injury."⁷

Taqiyya is a fundamental Islamic concept based on the Quran. The Quran holds blameless Muslims who disguise their beliefs in cases of safety.⁸ Mark Cohen adds:

---

⁵ Avraham Yaakov Finkel, trans., *Rabbi Yehudah HeChasid: Sefer Chasidim* (Northvale: Jason Aronson, 1997), 349-359.
⁶ Ibid., 349.
⁷ http://www.al-islam.org/encyclopedia/chapter6b/1.html
⁸ Qur'an 16:106.

> "Confronted by religious persecution, Muslims favored outward accommodation or dissimulation, in Arabic *taqiyya* while inwardly maintaining belief in Islam. Rather than having a Gentile model of martyrdom to emulate and even surpass, the Jews of Islam seem to have been influenced by the Islamic response to forced conversion in their own pattern of accommodation."[9]

Also, in all three Islamic persecutions of the medieval period, i.e., the persecution under al-Hakim, the Almohades, and the persecution in Yemen, Jews and Christians forcibly converted were eventually allowed to revert to their original faiths. The influence of *taqiyya* is evidenced in Maimonides' writings in response to forced conversions of Jews of Morocco and Yemen. Abdul Hamid Siddiqui refers to the words of Ibn Abbas, a Sunni commentator:

> "Al-Taqiyya is with the tongue only; he who has been coerced into saying that which angers Allah (SWT), and his heart is comfortable (i.e., his true faith has not been shaken.), then (saying that which he has been coerced to say) will not harm him (at all); (because) al-Taqiyya is with the tongue only, (not the heart)."[10]

Abdul Hamid Siddiqui also refers to Abd al-Razak, who in his book *Al- Dala-il* wrote:

> "The nonbelievers arrested 'Ammar Ibn Yasir and (tortured him until) he uttered foul words about the Prophet, and praised their gods (idols); and when they released him, he went straight to the Prophet. The Prophet said: 'Is there something on your mind?' 'Ammar Ibn Yasir said: 'Bad (news)! They would not release me until I defamed you

---

[9] Mark R. Cohen, *Under Crescent and Cross: The Jews in the Middle Ages* (Princeton: Princeton University Press, 1994), 176.
[10] http://www.al-islam.org/encyclopedia/chapter6b/1.html

and praised their gods!' The Prophet said: 'How do you find your heart to be?' `Ammar answered: 'Comfortable with faith.' So the Prophet said: 'Then if they come back for you, then do the same thing all over again.' Allah at that moment revealed the verse: '....except under compulsion, his heart remaining firm in faith... [16:106]'"[11]

Siddiqui also refers to what is narrated in al-Sirah al-Halabiyyah, v3, p. 61, that:

"After the conquest of the city of Khaybar by the Muslims, the Prophet was approached by Hajaj Ibn `Aalat and told: "O Prophet of Allah: I have in Mecca some excess wealth and some relatives, and I would like to have them back; am I excused if I bad-mouth you (to escape persecution)?' The Prophet excused him and said: 'Say whatever you have to say.'"[12]

Also, Alal al-Din al-Suyuti in his book, 'al-Durr al-Manthoor Fi al-Tafsir al-Ma'athoor,' v2, p. 176, narrates that:

"Abd Ibn Hameed, on the authority of al-Hassan, said: al-Taqiyya is permissible until the Day of judgment."[13]

Muhammad Ibn Sa'd, a Sunni scholar of the 9th century, in his book titled *al-Tabaqat al-Kubra*, relates the following on the authority of Ibn Sirin:

"The Prophet (S) saw `Ammar Ibn Yasir (ra) crying, so he (S) wiped off his (ra) tears, and said: "The nonbelievers arrested you and immersed you in water until you said such and such (i.e., bad-mouthing the Prophet (S) and

---

[11] Ibid.
[12] Ibid.
[13] Ibid.

praising the pagan gods to escape persecution); if they come back, then say it again."[14]

It is clear then that for Islam, the survival of a faithful Muslim is of utmost importance. The ability to feign loyalty to another religion is not considered problematic when faced with persecution.

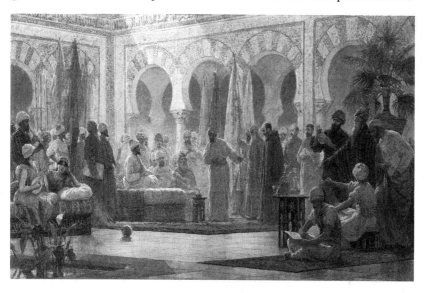

Abd-ar-Rahman III and his court receiving an ambassador in Medina Azahara, Còrdoba

The Fatwa of the Mufti of Oran

Despite the fall of the Kingdom of Granada in 1492, Muslims had nevertheless been guaranteed the freedom to observe Islam without restriction under Spanish rule. However, a rebellion at the end of the 15th century would serve as the pretext for the Spanish crown to issue an ultimatum regarding conversion to Christianity or expulsion.

---

[14]http://www.al-islam.org/shiite-encyclopedia-ahlul-bayt-dilp-team/al-taqiyya-dissimulation-part-1#reference-7

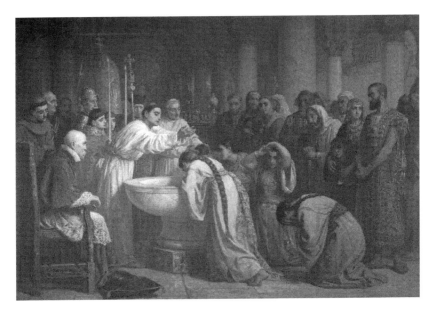

The Moorish Proselytes of Archbishop Ximenes, Granada, 1500

Like their Jewish counterparts, many Muslims opted for conversion as the most realistic option. However, the application of Taqiyya would receive a controversial but an official endorsement for these new converts known as Moriscos from the Mufti of Oran. In 1504, the Mufti issued a controversial *fatwa* to address the situation.

As Rosa Rodriguez notes, to survive the restraining structure of the Inquisition and secular authorities, Moriscos, like Conversos continuing to practice Judaism, were forced to hide their religious beliefs and masquerade all practices that would classify them as continuing to observe Islam. Rosa-Rodriguez summarizes the plight of Moriscos when states:

"Conversion meant that they were asked to commit blasphemy and curse Muhammad. They were also forced to break other tenets of Islam, such as eating foods forbidden by Islamic law. Because of this situation, crypto-Muslims (as well as crypto-Jews, Protestants, alumbrados, and other religious minorities) struggled with complicated religious dilemmas."[15]

Their situation would bring up many of the issues that Conversos also faced.

Burning of Jews in Portugal in 1497.

To what extent would Moriscos be allowed theologically to hide their faith was undoubtedly an issue of concern. Also, what elements of Islam could realistically be observed given the situation would have been of concern. The Mufti of Oran responded to these crypto-Muslims' issues in a *fatwa* that proved highly controversial outside of Spain. While rabbinic authorities issued no similar statement regarding Conversos who were practicing Judaism, the similarity in rabbinic responsa addressing specific issues related to Conversos can be seen.

The Mufti provided a striking response. He stated that Muslims were allowed to eat pork, drink wine, be baptized, recognize Jesus

---

[15] M.D.M. Rosa-Rodriguez, "Simulation and Dissimulation: Religious Hybridity in a Morisco Fatwa," Medieval Encounters 16 (2010): 143-180.

as the Son of God, and pray not as Rosa-Rodriguez points out according to Islamic doctrine, but at whatever time they were able and in whatever form they were able to pray. The critical issue was that the intention of their hearts remains directed towards Islam.[16]

The proper intention is a central theme throughout the *fatwa*, placing this above ritual concerns regarding importance. Rosa-Rodriguez explains that in Islam, the concept of *niyya* refers to intention, while *'amal* refers to an action. For the latter to be valid, proper *niyya* (or its parallel in Hebrew *kavannah*) must come first. The Mufti of Oran, however, cuts the bonds between these two complementary concepts. In effect, the Mufti argued that a Morisco could remain a Muslim without following normative Islamic practice or doctrine.

The Mufti addressed concerns over images and idols by dismissing them as nothing more than wood or stone. The Mufti cast off any aspersions that Christian images or idols maintained any significance. Any "honor" or homage given to them was void as the idols themselves were powerless.

> "Thus, I tell you that idols [idols are images of God and his saints] are not more than wood and stone, and there is no sense in them, nor the idols can [missing word] nor take advantage, and that all power is in God's will, who has not chosen a son, and there is another God in his side. Because of this, it would be honest and convenient thing to serve him, and constantly praise him with constant motivation and with great patience."[17]

---

[16] MS BRAH Gayangos n. 1922/36 (antiguo 28). Folio 344r refers to the subject of eating pork, drinking wine, and marriages. Folio 344v and 345r refers to the subject of Jesus and Mary. Folio 343v refers to issues regarding idols.

[17] English translation of the Fatwa: Epistola Mahometica del Apostata BRAH GAyangos n. 1922/36 (antiguo 28) f. 343r-346r

When presented with a requirement to confess Jesus as the Son of God, the Mufti offered Moriscos as a solution.

> "If they ask you to say that Jesus is the Son of God, you should confer that he is, and inside your hearts, you will say that he is a servant of Mary's God, truly adored. (folio 345r) and if they want you to say that Jesus is the Son of God, you will say that it with your mouth but inside your chest, you will keep a different opinion, and knowing the true God and that this house cannot be contaminated nor profaned."[18]

To a large extent, one can certainly argue that Islam had an easier time than Judaism in addressing issues of dissimulation as the former had already incorporated ideas from Christianity in its theology. Thus any references to Jesus or Mary, for example, could very easily be reconfigured into a form, less problematic than experienced by Judaism. However, the idea that dissimulation was an option was not so foreign to Iberian Jews.

Islamic ritual prescribes that one undergo ceremonial washing before engaging in prayer. Since this would draw attention, the Mufti suggested that Moriscos could instead rub against sand or stone as a means of purification before prayer.[19] To buttress his position, the Mufti referenced the words of Abin Hagio, who

---

"Muslim Letter from the Apostate" (folio 343r) in M.D.M. Rosa-Rodriguez, "Simulation and Dissimulation: Religious Hybridity in a Morisco Fatwa," Medieval Encounters 16 (2010) 176.

[18] Ibid., 178.

[19] Rosa-Rodriguez notes that using a stone to rub against instead of water is a sanctioned practice in Islam when water is not available. The typical scenario where this would be applied was during the desert or in a time of war. M.D.M. Rosa-Rodriguez, "Simulation and Dissimulation: Religious Hybridity in a Morisco Fatwa," Medieval Encounters 16, (2010):150.

quoted Mohammed stating, "Do whatever possibility allows you to do."[20] The Mufti's letter states:

> "And regarding the acala [prayer], I say that it should not be abandoned even if it is done with gestures and when the *acala* is disturbed during daytime do it at night time; in this manner, you will fulfill your obligation. And every time your enemies forcibly disturb the hours of the acala, making you go at these same times to their prayers and ceremonies to praise their idols, then your intention will be put in your hearts that you are praying the acala by our law and canon, without stopping to do what they do in front of their idols. Above all, seek the intention of your hearts is with God."[21]

Islamic practice allowed Muslims to marry their sons to Christian daughters since the latter were "Peoples of the Books." The reverse case of Morisco women marrying Christian men, however, was discouraged. When faced with the requirement to curse Muhammed, the Mufti suggested that Moriscos use slight grammatical changes or pronunciation to offset the intended imprecation.

> "If they ask you to blaspheme against Muhammad, which they call Mahoma, I tell you to say that blasphemy imagining that it is against a demon or a name used by the Jews or any other."[22]

---

[20] "Haced lo que la possibilidad os permita" MS quote BRAH Gayangos n. 1922/36 (antique 28) f. 344r.

[21] English translation of the Fatwa: Epistola Mahometica del Apostata BRAH Gayangos n. 1922/36 (antiguo 28) f. 343r-346r "Muslim Letter from the Apostate" (folio 343r) in M.D.M. Rosa-Rodriguez "Simulation and Dissimulation: Religious Hybridity in a Morisco Fatwa," Medieval Encounters 16, (2010):176.

[22] English translation of the Fatwa: Epistola Mahometica del Apostata BRAH GAyangos n. 1922/36 (antiguo 28) f. 343r-346r "Muslim Letter from the Apostate" (folio 343r) in M.D.M. Rosa-

In the end, the Mufti hoped that the expanding Ottoman Empire would reinstate Islamic rule in Spain. In essence, the Mufti was asking Moriscos to endure the short term in the hope of the day that would allow them to return openly to Islamic practice.[23] The Mufti's *fatwa* was contentious and rejected by many Muslims in Spain.

Other documents, such as the *fatwa* issued by Ahmad al-Wanshari, advised that all Moriscos leave Spain. Al-Wanshari's edict condemned those who stayed. They argued that practicing a religion clandestinely was not reflective of actual religious observance. These documents suggested that to save their souls, they should leave Spain or opt for martyrdom.[24]

Rodriguez, "Simulation and Dissimulation: Religious Hybridity in a Morisco Fatwa," Medieval Encounters 16 (2010): 178.

[23] Ibid.,151.

[24] See *fatwa* of Ahmad al-Wanshari cited in Abu al-Abbas Ahmad b. Yaha Al-Wanshari in Revista del Instituto Egiptcio de Estudios Islamicos en Madrid 5 (1957), 186-187. Additonal *fatwas* are available in K.A. Miller, "Muslim Minorities and the Obligations to Emmigrate to Islamic Territory: Two Fatwa/s from Fifteenth-Century Granada, "Islamic Law and Society 7 (2000): 256-288; P.S. Konigsveld and Gerard Wiegers, "The Islamic Statute of the Mudejars in the Light in the Light of a New Source." Al-Qantara 17.1 (1996): 19-58.

Expulsion of the Moriscos at the port of Dénia, by Vincente Mostre

The basis of support for the Mufti's position is, of course, the concept of *Taqiyya* already described. To revisit this theme, we only need to read the Quran to find the basic idea.

> "Whoever rejects his faith in Allah after having believed in Him- not the one who is compelled (to utter a word of disbelief) under duress while his heart is at peace with Faith, but the one who has laid his breast wide open for disbelief-upon such people is the wrath of Allah, and for them, there is a heavy punishment."[25]

In the end, many Moriscos remaining in Spain until their expulsion in the early 17th century only retained a fragile understanding of Islam, which as Rosa-Rodriguez notes, was often reduced to the Five Pillars of Islam.[26] Those Moriscos born during this

---

[25] Sura 16, verse 106. English translation by Mufti Muhammad Taqi Uthmami.

[26] M.D.M. Rosa-Rodriguez "Simulation and Dissimulation: Religious Hybridity in a Morisco Fatwa," Medieval Encounters 16, (2010):155

period experienced a dissimulated structure of Islam, which was characterized by an overlap of Christian practices and Islamic overtones and subjective beliefs.[27] This is something that would be the same case for crypto-Jews.

---

[27] Ibid., 148.

CHAPTER 6

Maimonides' Response to Persecution

The rise of the Almohades (*Al-Muwahhidun*: those who assert the unity of God) in Northwest Africa and Spain in the 12th century initiated a period of forced conversions. Many Jews were forced to give a public confession that Mohammad was the prophet of God. Others refused to do so and died as martyrs. A distinctive element of the Almohade persecution lay in the fact that the Almohades appear to have only required the recitation of the *shahad,* a statement testifying the prophethood of Mohammed. They did not actively alter behavior in private domains. Maimonides' own family was affected by the persecution. They traveled extensively in an attempt to escape the onslaught.

In the aftermath of the persecutions, controversy arose on how these forced converts should be received in the Jewish community and what they should do if they lived in the lands subject to the Almohades. One rabbi had responded quite forcefully that in proclaiming Mohammed as a prophet, they had professed idolatry. He appealed to the Talmudic dictum that "Whoever professes idolatry is as if he denied the entire Torah."[1] However, some of the forced converts were secretly continuing their Jewish observance. Despite this, the rabbi dismissed the validity or efficacy

---

[1] Bavli Nedarim 28a; Bavli Kiddushin 40a.

of any observance performed by this *anusim* by stating that any commandment they observed would be counted against them as a transgression.

> "If one of the forced converts enters one of their houses and worship, even if he does not say a word, and he then goes home and offers his prayers, his prayer is charged against him as an added sin and transgression."[2]

Learning of the rabbi's response to one of the forced converts in question, Rabbi Moses ben Maimon angrily sought to dismiss what he saw as a foolish and disgraceful reply. Maimonides began by arguing that the rabbi did not understand the difference between a voluntary transgressor and a forced one. Nowhere in the Torah argued Maimonides, was there any indication that a forced individual was sentenced to any punishment, regardless of the severity of the transgression. The only individual who was subject to punishment was the voluntary transgressor. Maimonides appealed to the biblical verse which states

> "But the person …who acts defiantly…that soul shall be cut off."[3]

He also referenced the Talmud, which states,

> "The Torah rules that the forced individual is not culpable, for this case is like that of a man attacking another and murdering him [Deuteronomy 22:26]."[4]

The Talmud also affirmed that the forced convert was not dubbed as a transgressor or wicked. The forced convert was also not disqualified from giving testimony, except when the forced convert

---

[2] David Hartman, *Crisis and Leadership: Epistles of Maimonides* (Philadelphia: Jewish Publication Society, 1985), 16.
[3] Numbers 15:30.
[4] Bavli Nedarim 27a.

had committed an offense that made him ineligible from serving as a witness.⁵

Maimonides was particularly critical of the rabbi's attitude in condemning forced converts for not having opted for martyrdom.

18ᵗʰ-century depiction of Moses ben Maimon

Maimonides appealed to various Scriptural and midrashic sources to argue that the rabbi's character assassination of these forced converts was unacceptable. He appealed that before the Exodus, most Israelites except Levi's tribe had failed to observe the commandment of circumcision and that many had even fallen into depravity. Referencing Ezekiel 23:2, the rabbis interpreted that

---

⁵ Bavli Bava Kamma 72b and Bavli Sanhedrin 27a.

Israel had even practiced incest. Despite their corruption, the rabbis argued that God rebuked Moses when he questioned,

> " 'What if they do not believe in me? [Exodus 4:1].' God replied that the Israelites were '...believers, children of believers...' as Scripture reports: '...and the people... believed [Exodus 14:31]; sons of believers: because he believed, He reckoned it to his merit [Genesis 15:6].'"[6]

The same was the case during the Prophet Elijah's escape to Mount Sinai in the aftermath of the confrontation with Baal and Asherah's prophets. In relating the fact that Israel had fallen into idolatry, Elijah is confronted with a retort by God that it would have been more reasonable to direct his accusations against the Gentiles.[7] Maimonides' point is clear that the rabbi's attitude and critique of the forced converts, whatever their failure, was wrong and misplaced.

To dismiss the rabbi's argument that forced converts living publically as Gentiles, despite their secret Jewish observance, were, in fact, Gentiles, Maimonides appealed to the account of no less a scholar such as Rabbi Meir and Rabbi Eliezer practicing dissimulation to survive persecution. Maimonides states:

> "It is common knowledge that in the course of a persecution during which Jewish sages were executed, Rabbi Meir was arrested. Some who knew him said: 'You are Meir, aren't you?' and he replied: 'I am not.' Pointing to ham, they ordered: 'eat this if you are not Jewish.' He responded: 'I shall readily eat it,' and he pretended he was eating, but did not, in fact."[8]

---

[6] Bavli Shabbat 97a and Exodus Rabbah 3:12.

[7] David Hartman, *Crisis and Leadership: Epistles of Maimonides* (Philadelphia: Jewish Publication Society, 1985), 18.

[8] Ibid., 20.

In Rabbi Eliezer's case, he was accused of heresy, which Maimonides claimed was even worse than idolatry. When asked how an accomplished man of science could believe in religion, Rabbi Eliezer answered in a manner that appeared to give credence to his inquisitors' critique. Maimonides notes that while his answer seemed to support their views, Rabbi Eliezer was, in fact, "thinking of the true religion and no other." The issue is clear. Rabbi Eliezer pretended to be a heretic while retaining his genuine belief in God. Maimonides sought to demonstrate that despite their seeming failure when faced with persecution, repentance was always available to the sincere individual. To illustrate this, Maimonides noted that even the wicked King Ahab had humbled himself, and God was merciful to him.

> "It is explicitly reported in the Bible that Ahab son of Omri who denied God and worshipped idols, as God attests: 'Indeed there never was anyone like Ahab [I Kings 21:25], had the decree against him rescinded after he fasted two and a half hours. The Bible informs us: 'Then the word of the LORD came to Elijah the Tishbite: 'Have you seen how Ahab has humbled himself before Me. Because He has humbled himself before Me, I will not bring the disaster in his lifetime; I will bring the disaster upon his house in his son's time [I Kings 21:28-29].'"[9]

Maimonides argued that God rewarded every individual for the good deeds they performed, as well as punishing those who continued to commit transgressions. He argued the following to buttress his view that forced converts who continued to observe the commandments would be rewarded. If God rewarded someone as wicked as Ahab after repenting, honored King Eglon of Moab for having risen to hear the word of the LORD, and granted Esau dominion until the Messianic era because he paid homage to his

---

[9] Ibid., 22.

father, God would undoubtedly honor those who endeavored to keep the commandments despite their forced conversions.[10]

Maimonides was aware that the situation facing Jews under the Almohade persecution was unique since all they required was a "profession of faith." In his letter, Maimonides noted that Rabbi Dime ruled in the name of Rabbi Yochanan that even if it was not a time of persecution, an individual should only transgress instead of undergoing martyrdom in private. In public, Rabbi Dimi ruled that even violating a minor rabbinic enactment was prohibited. A public violation was defined as in front of ten Israelites.[11] Profanation of God's name was a grave sin for which unintentional sinners and premeditated sinners were punished. Maimonides sought to encourage those facing persecutions to flee as soon as possible to avoid profaning God's name. The realities of life and the likelihood of not everyone being able to meet were not lost on him. Maimonides declared the following.

> "Anyone who cannot leave because of his attachments, or because of the dangers of a sea voyage, and stays where he is, must look upon himself as one who profanes God's name, not exactly willingly, but almost so. At the same time, he must bear in mind that if he fulfills a precept, God will reward him doubly because he acted so for God only and to show off or be accepted as an observant individual. The reward is much greater for a person who fulfills the Law and knows that if he is caught, he and all he has will perish. It is he who is meant in God's qualification: 'If only you seek Him with all your heart and soul [Deuteronomy 4:29]'. Nevertheless, no one should stop to plan to leave the provinces that God is wroth with, and to exert every effort to achieve it."[12]

---

[10] Ibid., 23.
[11] Bavli Sanhedrin 74a.
[12] David Hartman, *Crisis and Leadership: Epistles of Maimonides* (Philadelphia: Jewish Publication Society, 1985), 33.

Maimonides extolled martyrdom's virtues by noting the sacrifice that Hananiah, Mishael, and Azariah were willing to endure when compelled to worship Nebuchadnezzar's idol. He also noted the case of Daniel, the apocryphal story of Hannah, and the case of the Ten Martyrs.

A person, whom Maimonides described as meriting the privilege of ascending to this rank, even if he or she had been wicked, would surely merit the world to come. Nevertheless, Maimonides was quite aware of the realities of most individual's spiritual levels. For those who failed the test of martyrdom and opted to transgress to preserve their lives, Maimonides stated the following:

> "Now if he did not surrender himself to death but transgressed under duress and did not die, he did not act properly, and under compulsion, he profaned God's name. However, he is not to be punished by any of the seven means of retribution. Not a single instance is found in the Torah in which a forced individual is sentenced to any of the punishments, whether the transgression was light or grave..."[13]

In this particular case and in Maimonides' letter to Yemen's community who underwent similar persecution, the fact that Islam was not considered idolatrous was undoubtedly helpful in applying this lenient view. Also, since the conversion to Islam under the Almohades only required a recitation and not more extensive actions typical of Christian practices, leniency could be more readily extended. Islamic practice was also much closer to Judaism than Christianity was, which allowed for a higher degree of obscurity when practicing Jewish customs in the case of Maimonides' letters to affected communities. Mark Cohen states:

> "Jews could accept Islam outwardly, demonstrating their conversion by attending Friday prayer and

---

[13] Ibid., 29.

> avoiding acts disapproved of in Islam, while secretly adhering to Judaism in the privacy of their homes."[14]

At least one Islamic source of the 10th century upholds that the forced conversion is not binding unless the convert has overcome their fear.[15] Maimonides rejected the view that if a Jew could not observe all the commandments, then partial observance has no significance.[16] Maimonides believed that God valued every commandment performed by a repentant individual.

> "Maimonides addressed the Jewish status of these individuals by first noting the fact the Bible's own depiction of Israel's history. For Maimonides, the argument was simple. If the generation that had experienced the exodus from Egypt as well as the associated miracles had fallen into idolatry but were still called Israel, the same approach should be extended to individuals that had yielded to violent persecution and transgressed unwillingly."[17]

Maimonides noted that in ancient Israel when the prophets condemned Jews, it was because they worshiped Baal voluntarily. David Hartman relates:

> "Had the Almohads required Jews to participate in Islamic rituals and practices, and had they forbidden Jewish observances in private, then the consequences of such behavioral conditioning would constitute a much greater

---

[14] Mark R. Cohen, *Under Crescent and Cross: The Jews in the Middle Ages* (Princeton: Princeton University Press, 1994), 176.

[15] Ibid., 176.

[16] David Hartman, *Crisis and leadership: Epistles of Maimonides* (Jewish Publication Society, 1985), 95.

[17] "A Jew always remains responsible to Halakhah and obligated to perform mitzvoth, regardless of his past sins." David Hartman, *Crisis and leadership: Epistles of Maimonides* (Jewish Publication Society, 1985), 95.

threat to the community than the simple recitation of a faith formula."[18]

In his letter's most striking passage, Maimonides argued that martyrdom was unnecessary in this case since it only concerned a verbal acceptance and not a change in religious practice. The Almohades, for all their zeal, were purportedly not determined to investigate behavior outside of the public domain. Maimonides stated:

> "But if anyone comes to ask me whether to surrender his life or acknowledge, I tell him to confess and not choose death. However, he should not continue to live in the domain of that ruler. He should stay home and not go out, and if he is dependent on his work, let him be the Jew in private. There has never been persecution as remarkable as this one where the only coercion is to say something."[19]

Maimonides continues his letter by counseling his readers to make every effort to leave the land of persecution. Maimonides urged his readers to leave these lands and journey to a place where they could practice Judaism freely. However, Maimonides also advocated his readers to leave their family and home and all their possessions if necessary. This position appears at odds with his earlier statement regarding those who stayed because of their livelihoods. Maimonides was engaged in a tough balancing act attempting to assuage those who remained while simultaneously challenging them not to be complacent in their situation. To note the seriousness of not escaping, he referred to the Talmudic statement regarding those who dwelt outside the land of Israel as equivalent to those who denied the existence of God. His exile notwithstanding, he referred to the prophets to prove his point.

> "Indeed, the prophets have spelled out that a person who resides among nonbelievers is one of them."[20]

---

[18] Ibid., 85.
[19] Ibid., 30.
[20] Bavli Ketubot 110b.

Despite the critical nature of the passage, it is also clear that the individual's halakhic status did not change by their failure to depart. Failing to flee rendered the forced convert a transgressor, a profaner of God's name, and "almost a presumptuous sinner." They were not to be turned away and rejected. To illustrate this, Maimonides referred to the case of the Shabbat desecrator. He stated that it was not correct to alienate, scorn, or hate those who violated the Shabbat. It was the duty of faithful Jews to make friends with and encourage them to fulfill the commandments. Maimonides states:

> "The rabbis regulate explicitly that when an evil-doer who sinned by choice comes to the synagogue, he is to be welcomed and not insulted."[21]

If a willful sinner was accepted without reservation, the forced convert failed to immediately comply with the directive to flee the land of persecution was also to be received without impediment.

The differences between Christianity and Islam bring up issues in the letter's applicability to the case of Conversos in the 14th and 15th centuries. Maimonides relates the severity of idolatry when he states:

> "A Jew who commits idolatry is considered as a gentile in all respects, and not like a Jew who has committed some other sin which carries a penalty of stoning. A convert to [the ways of] idolatry is considered as an apostate. Similarly, a Jewish infidel is not considered as a Jew in all respects and is never accepted in repentance, for it is written, 'None that go to her return, nor do they regain the paths of life.' Infidels are those who follow the impulses of their hearts with respect to the aforementioned matters, so much so that they transgress the key commandments of the Torah

---

[21] David Hartman, *Crisis and Leadership: Epistles of Maimonides* (Jewish Publication Society, 1985), 33.

in contempt and brazenness, and they will say that they are not sinning. It is forbidden to converse with them or make them repent at all, for it is written, '...and don't approach the door of her house.' The thoughts of a heretic are keyed to idolatry."[22]

A review of selected rabbinic responsa shows that some Conversos did face circumstances in which a superficial acquiescence to Christianity was all was required or even expected. This particularly true in the period following the initial violence of 1391. I believe many Conversos knew that the authorities' vigilance varied considerably. Open expressions of Jewish observance were undoubtedly problematic, but discrete or private if not public associations were not as difficult until the intensification and redirection of the Inquisitions towards Judaizing and relapsing converts was made.

Also, I believe that knowing that Maimonides had fundamentally justified the actions of those who had converted to Islam may have influenced Jews in the 14th and 15th centuries. Rabbi Isaac ben Sheshet applied this view in his response on the matter of *anusim*. There were without question significant disparities between Christianity and Islam. Unlike Islam, Christianity was wrought with religious imagery, which for most Jews constituted idolatry. At least in the early years, many Conversos could continue Jewish observances in their homes undisturbed. Maimonides' letter was referenced in later rabbinic responsa regarding Conversos, which shows that the rabbis did apply the letter's views to the present-day occurrences. Whether in fact, Conversos retained fidelity to Judaism in "their hearts" is what Benzion Netanyahu and Norman Roth argue against. While we cannot know the personal reasons that each Jew opted for conversion were, the individual Converso may have gambled that an eventual

---

[22] MT Hilchot Teshuvah 3:5.

allowance of religious behavior may have been allowed to return sometime in the future.

CHAPTER 7

The Collapse of Faith

We have already briefly reviewed the opinion that philosophy and rationalism played a significant role in the demise of Jewish fidelity to Judaism in the 14th and 15th centuries. While supported by four contemporary Jewish writers, the problem with this position lies in the simple fact that no record of any notable Jewish philosophers converting or abandoning Judaism exists. Suppose the philosophical movement had indeed been the primary component of Jewish communal collapse. In that case, it might be expected that at least some noted Jewish philosophers would have converted to Christianity. In response to this, Allan and Helen Culter offer the following scenario:

> "The majority of the Jewish Aristotelians in fourteenth-century Spain did not carry their philosophical beliefs out to their ultimate conclusions. But a small minority did, and this minority apparently exerted an increasing influence upon the Jewish upper class..."[1]

---

[1] Allan Harris Cutler and Helen Elmquist Cutler, *The Jews as Ally of the Muslim: Medieval Roots of Anti-Semitism* (Notre Dame: University of Notre Dame, 1986), 272.

Who these philosophers were is not clear. Cutler and Cutler also offer a series of reasons why Jewish communal life collapsed at the end of the 14th century and well into the 15th century. Their possible explanations range from Spanish Jewry's strong power drive, the impact of the Spanish civil war, the role of philosophy, the role of mysticism, and the belief in reincarnation. What is clear, I believe, is that the internal makeup of the Jewish community changed radically regarding its leadership. Philosophy and mysticism certainly played a role in this decline, but not in a manner they are typically assumed to have.

The rise of the Converso phenomena is partly connected to the undermining of Jewish religious institutions. According to Jose Faur, the rise of the anti-Maimonidean movement and the changing nature of rabbinic leadership in the Iberian Peninsula led to the gradual collapse of Jewish communal life and leadership. The prevailing view also holds that the anti-Maimonidean forces held the line against assimilationist trends engendered by the rationalistic and philosophic camps of the pro-Maimonideans.[2] The anti-

---

[2] Yitzhak Baer, *A History of the Jews in Christian Spain*, Volume 1 (Philadelphia; Jewish Publication Society, 1961), 96-110. In response to the commonly held views that philosophical speculation was a key determining factor in the eventual apostasy of Iberian Jewry, Jose Faur writes: "Responding to their own intellectual and spiritual bent, modern historians non-chalantly dismissed the preceding sources and the implications therein. Because of their own agenda, too painful to be analyzed in this paper, modern historians refrained from pointing out the connection between the triumph of the anti-Maimonideans, the rise of Kabbalah, the spread of pietistic doctrines, and the decay of Jewish learning and Jewish leadership in Spain, leading to mass conversions, and the Expulsion in 1492. Ever since Yitzhak Baer, it had become a truism that Jewish apostasy was the result of 'secular acculturation,' i.e., the adoption of the traditional values of old Sepharad- 'Averroism' in particular." Moses Lazar and

Maimonidean forces are generally considered the authentic expression of Judaism.

In his article, *Anti- Maimonidean Demons,* Jose Faur notes the simple point that the mass apostasy to Christianity took place after and not before the attack on Maimonides. This is a point ignored mainly by those blaming the impact of philosophical speculation on those who converted. Conversely, one may argue that Faur's contention that the radical change in Jewish leadership and philosophical outlook in the Peninsula set the stage for the conversions should be muted since they occurred two hundred years after.

Instead, Faur contends that the opposite is true. The anti-Maimonidean forces, far from embracing a more authentic Jewish expression, were reflective of assimilation of prevailing Christian attitudes towards philosophy and humanistic studies. Faur states:

> "Unknowingly, the anti-Maimonideans promoted Christian ideology. It should be emphasized that they were not conscious of their mental assimilation. Their opposition fostered the illusion of total autonomy, barring an analysis of the basic elements affecting their own thinking process."[3]

Perhaps the most controversial aspect of Jose Faur's proposition is as follows:

Stephen Haliczer, Eds. *The Jews of Spain and the Expulsion of 1492* (Lancaster: Labyrinthos, 1997), 45.

[3] Jose Faur, *In the Shadow of History: Jews and Conversos at the Dawn of Modernity* (New York: SUNY, 1992), 1. See also Jose Faur, "Anti-Maimonidean Demons," *Review of Rabbinic Judaism* 6 (2003): 3-52.

> "A mark of the anti-Maimonidean ideology (whereby zeal displaces halakhah) is the sanction of violence as a legitimate means for the implementation of 'religion.'"

Among the principal characteristics of the contemporary Christian society was the persecution of heterodox minority communities. Persecution became a major component of Christian ideology. In the Jewish community, the anti-Maimonidean circles harassed Jews who favored other approaches to Jewish thought other than their own and created a distinct group marked for persecution.[4] The consequences of these actions cannot be underestimated as Jose Faur notes:

> "One need not be particularly bright to have realized that requesting the Dominicans to burn Maimonides' works established an extremely dangerous precedent."[5]

The Undermining of Religious Institutions

The trend resulted in the loss of the creativity characteristic of Iberian Jewish life centuries before. Intellectual life in its scientific, humanistic, and diplomatic life ended or at least declined. Alienation of the lay elite occurred. The loss of creative leadership was felt when anti-Semitic riots of the 14th and 15th centuries were experienced.[6] Faur argues that opposition to the

---

[4] Jose Faur, *In the Shadow of History: Jews and Conversos at the Dawn of Modernity* (New York: SUNY, 1992), 2.

[5] Jose Faur, "Anti-Maimonidean Demons," *Review of Rabbinic Judaism* 6 (2003): 3-52.

[6] The only venue for continued "Jewish" creativity in the intellectual sphere was in Christian circles, though these circles were often narrow as well. Noting Americo Castro, Jose Faur states: "Most of all creative thinking in the sciences, humanities, and literature in Spain was the product of Conversos. And yet nothing similar was taking place within Jewish communities. It was only in modern times, when Jews were able to function

Maimonidean tradition was ultimately founded upon Christian thought patterns. It reflected the religious tradition of the Christian Bernard of Clairvaux rather than Talmudic tradition.[7]

The other primary internal reason critical to the Converso phenomena' rise is the changing of religious leadership in Spain, which led to a spiritual vacuum and diplomatic ineptitude when a crisis arose.[8] The intellectual and religious life of Jews in the Iberian Peninsula had previously reflected a religious tradition that was based upon the idea of a pluralistic society of Andalusia, where Christian, Moorish, and Jewish scholars worked next to one another to transmit the classics rediscovered and produced by Islamic schools. Jewish life until the Maimonidean era was structured because the Torah's commandments were regulated by precise legislation and not by impulsive religious zeal. As Rabbi Judah Ha-Levi had noted, the commandments had precisely known definitions. They functioned as the ultimate categories of Judaism.[9]

The anti-Maimonidean forces' greatest champion was Rabbi Solomon Montpelier. The anti-Maimonidean movement attempted to establish the domination of the "French Rabbis" into the Iberian Peninsula. This is exhibited in the words of Rabbi Joseph ben Todros Ablu'afya, who was among the first Iberian

---

outside of their community, that Jewish creativity flourished, and scientific and humanistic knowledge became possible. Thus, the Converso phenomenon was the result of internal, as well as external, causes." Jose Faur, *In the Shadow of History: Jews and Conversos at the Dawn of Modernity* (New York: SUNY, 1992), 2.

[7] Ibid. 12.

[8] Norman Roth, *Conversos, Inquisition, and the Expulsion of the Jews from Spain* (Madison: University of Wisconsin, 1995), 13.

[9] David H. Baneth, *The Kuzari* (Jerusalem: Hebrew University Press, 1977), 129.

rabbis to rail against those who supported Maimonidean perspectives. He reproached those who did for their rejection of "our French Rabbis" and for their not "follow[ing] in the footsteps of the sages of the Kabbalah."[10]

Those who rejected Kabbalah were characterized as undermining "the foundations of the Kabbalah." More seriously, they were painted as having rebelled against God for their failure to adopt Kabbalistic theology. The Maimonideans were warned that no one "should either rebel against the Almighty or confront the sages of Kabbalah." The reason was clear. The French rabbis were trustworthy and were designated as those,

> "from whose waters we drink, and in all the confines of the land, we live by their mouth."[11]

There were others like Rabbi Jonah of Girona who, in his zeal, was willing to collaborate with the Church to ensure the confiscation and destruction of some of Moses Ben Maimonides' works. In a letter written to Rabbi Judah Al-Fakhkhar of Toledo, who led the anti-Maimonidean movement there, Rabbi David Qamhi wrote the following:

> "My intention is not to denounce your or debate with you, but to apprise you as to whom you have chosen and proclaimed to be righteous, wise, and unblemished. Whereas, in fact, he [R. Jonah] is evil and unlearned, since he has passed into wickedness, perverted his ways, and became an informer and enemy collaborator. Thus, his following actions revealed the purpose of his earlier actions. May the heavens reveal his sin and the earth rise against him! Because when he had realized that the Rabbis in France had rejected him and regarded him as an unlearned person, and recognized him as the bearer of false testimony,

---

[10] Moses Lazar, and Stephen Haliczer, Eds. *The Jews of Spain and the Expulsion of 1492* (Lancaster: Labyrinthos, 1997), 41.
[11] Ibid., 42.

he turned to the graven images and idol worshipers [i.e., the Church], and implored of them and they consented to assist him since he was denouncing the Jews. First, he went to the Franciscans telling them: 'Look, most of our people are heretics and unbelievers, because they were duped by R. Moses of Egypt [Maimonides] who wrote heretical books. You exterminate your heretics, also exterminate ours!' Thereafter, they ordered the burning of those books, which were the Book of Knowledge (the first part of the Mishne Torah and the Guide. His uncircumcised heart, however, did not rest until he also told the same words to the Dominicans and the clergy. Finally, the words reached the Cardinal [Romanus]. Consequently, the Jews in Montpelier and those associated with them fell into grave danger, becoming the ridicule and scorn of the Gentiles. This heinous slanderer went out from town to town, saying: 'Look! The Law of the Jews is finished, since they had become two sects, and there is no other religion except for our own religion."[12]

Rabbi Al-Fakhkhar responded to Rabbi Qamhi's letter. He noted that Rabbi Solomon of Montpelier had authorized Rabbi Jonah to act accordingly to bring about "the vengeance of the LORD." Rabbi Jonah was therefore justified in approaching the Church and in the eventual burning of Maimonides' works. Rabbi Al-Fakhkhar argued that,

> "He had saved the Holy Writings from your fire." To save Judaism from the errors of Maimonidean philosophy, Rabbi Jonah's actions were acceptable. So convinced was Rabbi Al-Fakhkhar of the danger of

---

[12] Rabbi Qamhi's views were supported by Rabbi Abraham ibn Hasdai. Moses Lazar and Stephen Haliczer, Eds. *The Jews of Spain and the Expulsion of 1492* (Lancaster: Labyrinthos, 1997), 42.

Maimonides' philosophical teachings, that he described the Guide to the Perplexed as follows: "It [the Guide] warrants burning...and the fire upon the altar was devouring it [the Guide], in order that the children of Israel should not prostitute after it."[13]

Decades later, Rabbi Solomon Montpelier, Rabbi Jonah, and Rabbi Al-Fakhkhar were joined by other noteworthy rabbis in their struggle against Maimonides' philosophical interpretations. Rabbi Solomon ben Aderet issued a ban against Maimonideans in Barcelona on July 26, 1305. His view on the matter is expressed in the following:

> "...because in that city are those who write iniquity about the Tora, and if there would be a heretic writing books, they should be burnt as if they were the books of sorcerers."[14]

Rabbi Asher ben Yehiel was initially from Germany. He became the leader of the Jewish community of Toledo and supported the anti-Maimonidean position. In writing to Rabbi Israel de Toledo, secretary of the Court, he noted his opposition to philosophical inquiry.

> "But the science of philosophy is natural, and they [the sages of old Sepharad] were very wise, and determined every item according to its nature. But from so much

---

[13] Moses Lazar and Stephen Haliczer, Eds. *The Jews of Spain and the Expulsion of 1492* (Lancaster: Labyrinthos, 1997), 43.

[14] Rabbi Aderet would also write: "Go into the far lands inhabited by the Canaanites [an allusion to the Christians], and all the gentiles would have punished them [the Maimonideans] as heretics even for a single heresy or abomination that they had written in their books...and they would have lied them with up with brances and incinerated them till they turn to powder." Moses Lazar and Stephen Haliczer, Eds. *The Jews of Spain and the Expulsion of 1492* (Lancaster: Labyrinthos, 1997), 43-44.

wisdom, they went deep, and they became corrupt. And they were forced to repudiate the Law of Moses because all the Law is not natural...And whoever would enter from the beginning in this science [philosophy] would never be able to escape from it and to bring into his heart the science of the Law...And consequently, he would twist the Law because they are mutually exclusive and are not compatible with one another."[15]

It was Rabbi Moses ben Nachman, who ultimately reflected a new form of Jewish orthodoxy deeply rooted in emerging Kabbalistic thought. It strongly opposed the philosophical inclinations so reflective of Maimonides and other Jewish philosophers and halachists. Rabbi Moses ben Nachman's approach to both the basis of rabbinic authority and an understanding of Jewish law observance was radically different from that of his predecessors. It arguably subordinated halakhah to Kabbalah.[16]

It is also not merely an issue of the growing importance of Kabbalah, but of specific ideas like reincarnation that may have

---

[15] Moses Lazar and Stephen Haliczer, Eds. *The Jews of Spain and the Expulsion of 1492* (Lancaster: Labyrinthos, 1997), 48. Jose Faur also argues that the rabbis from France and Germany adopted a totalitarian approach to halakhah even in matters that were not associated with the issue of philosophy. He points to the case of Rabbi Jacob of Valencia. Rabbi Jacob had prohibited the use of a public avenue on the Sabbath unless a physical door was affixed to one of its entry points. Rabbi Solomon Ben Aderet had maintained the same view on the mater. Rabbi Asher disagreed with Rabbi Jacob's position and threatened to excommunicate him unless he repudiated his position. Rabbi Asher wrote that unless he relented "I am excommunicating you. If you would have been at the time of the Sanhedrin they would have put you to death." Ibid., 49.

[16] Jose Faur, *Anti-Maimonidean Demons,* Netanya College, 20.

played an influential role in Spanish Jewish society. While the idea of reincarnation exists in the *Bahir* and the *Zohar*, they represented limited forms of this concept. They did not per the views of Moses De Leon. Isaac ibn Latif includes the idea that reincarnation was the primary means of divine retribution. Interestingly, Shem Tov ben Shem Tov, one of the individuals who blamed philosophy as the principal reason for the mass conversion, in his *Sefer Ha-Emunot* proposed reincarnation as the primary means of divine reward and punishment. That reincarnation would undermine the adherence to Jewish law is not definitive but does raise a complicated scenario. Cutler and Cutler state:

> "Rather, the way God punished the sinner was by temporarily bringing his soul back again in a lower form of life. But if in this subsequent earthly life the sinner behaved, he could rise up the ladder of rebirth and come back as a person again in his next reincarnation. Thus, punishment for sin was not eternal, and punishment for the ultimate sin of apostasy was also not eternal. Such being the case, why should the Jews not convert en masse…"[17]

It is an issue worth noting and remarkably would become a point of contention between the rabbis of the Amsterdam Sephardic community of the 17th century composed almost entirely of former Conversos. As we will see in a subsequent chapter, the head rabbi of the community, Rabbi Saul Levi Morteira, would contend that belief in reincarnation rather than eternal punishment prevented Conversos from leaving the domains of idolatry since they believed they still could enjoy a place in the World to Come, albeit after several reincarnations. Norman Roth supports the view that Kabbalah played a significant component. He states:

> "There is, therefore, no question but that the fifteenth century saw a complete breakdown and virtual collapse of the

---

[17] Allan Harris Cutler and Helen Elmquist Cutler, *The Jews as Ally of the Muslim: Medieval Roots of Anti-Semitism* (Notre Dame: University of Notre Dame, 1986), 281.

high level of Jewish learning which had characterized Spanish Jewry from the earliest days. The vacuum was filled, to the extent that it was, not by Baer's nemesis, philosophy, but by its opponent qabalah....all these factors paved the way for the final chapter, which saw the conversion of undoubtedly the majority of Jews of Spain before the Expulsion was decreed."[18]

In short, Rabbi Moses ben Nachman's approach posited him as a harsh critic of the rationalism previously hitherto known in Andalusian Jewish communities. The issue is not the validity of Nachman's views but rather the radically different approaches and antagonism that arose against what had been the mainstay of Jewish life for centuries. The philosophically and nationalistically leaning approaches of prior years were over. Rabbi Moses ben Nachman's redirection in rabbinic thought was not merely one focused towards the mystical.

According to Jose Faur, a complete transformation of the halakhic foundations that had been characteristic before of Judaism before. According to Faur, Nachman no longer recognized the Torah as the singular constitutive of the human relationship with God. Commenting on the Torah, Rabbi Moses ben Nachman argued that one could be depraved within the boundaries of the Torah. While this might seem to be a call toward a higher level of righteousness, it repositioned the Torah's authority. Nachman indicated that a higher decisive factor was needed to achieve the holiness reflected in Leviticus 19:2. Nachman stated, "such as abstention from the pollution that although it was not forbidden to us by the Law." In effect, he argued that perfection transcends the commandments of the Torah.

However, the Andalusian tradition had reflected the views of Rabbi Judah ha-Levi, who had argued that the commandments

---

[18] Norman Roth, *Conversos, Inquisition, and the Expulsion of the Jews from Spain* (Madison: University of Wisconsin, 1995), 13.

have precisely known definitions that functioned as the ultimate categories of Judaism. According to this view, Jews were to follow the divine will by living "according to its definitions and stipulations."[19] The "it" in question was the Torah, which was definite and composed of precise legal definitions. Personal instinct and wisdom were not the factors determining Israel's religious obligations. The above factors were representative of elements within the concept of *itjihad,* meaning personal endeavor.

The most revealing example of *itjihad* was the biblical example of Israel worshipping the golden calf. Israel's sin was not worshipping another God, but worshipping God according to *itjihad.* In Rabbi Judah ha-Levi's work titled the *Kuzari,* the pagan King is introduced as a diligent and good man (*yujtahad*) in his religious observance. An angel appears to him and reveals that though his intentions were good, his actions were not. The goal of ha-Levi's *Kuzari* was the repudiation of the concept of *itjihad.* Another example is Nadav and Abihu, Aaron's sons, who presented strange incense in the tabernacle. The act itself may have been an act of personal zeal, but outside of the Torah's prescribed boundaries.[20]

Rabbi Judah Ha-Levi's goal was arguably not eliminating zeal or passion from Jewish worship. Rather, it was the restraint of its application concerning the Torah. The restraint of *itjihad* was, in fact, a significant distinction between Judaism and other religious traditions. Judaism was grounded on the Torah's revelation at Sinai. The personal endeavor was present in Jewish tradition but was subordinate to the distinct categories of the Torah.

Other religious traditions, however, were founded on *itjihad.* If personal endeavors were accepted as a decisive spiritual factor, no distinction between heathenism, magic, or any religious creed

---

[19] Jose Faur, *In the Shadow of History: Jews and Conversos at the Dawn of Modernity*, (New York: SUNY, 1992), 10.
[20] Ibid.,11.

would exist. Rabbi Moses ben Nachman, Faur argues, epitomized the embrace of *itjihad* by various Spanish and French rabbis. He argued that rabbis' authority to legislate was not predetermined in the Torah. Consequently, another source, independent of the Torah, must determine man's obligations towards God.

Nachmanides rejected Maimonides' view that what could be inferred from the Torah was the Torah itself. Instead, it maintained that whatever was derived from personal intuition and study was explicitly ordered by the Torah. Incidentally, this rejection of Maimonides' position was also a refutation of Judah ha-Levi's notion of an "alien cult."[21] However, the most significant differentiation in Nachmanides and Maimonides' approach was not merely the former's anti-rationalism, but his belief in and interest in the "the science of necromancy." In a critical passage, Nachmanides argued that rationalism could be disregarded on the evidence of necromancy.[22] The fact that Nachmanides viewed necromancy as a basis for seeing rationalism as futile opposed the views of Maimonides, who viewed sorcery and witchcraft as lies and falsehood. Nachmanides went as far as opposing the

---

[21] Jose Faur argues that a primary example of Nachmanides' position is his rejection of the Maimonidean view that prayer was a biblical commandment. "Since prayer are not part of the Sinaitic pact, and since rabbinic authority is not biblical, it follows that prayers are a purely human institution- a form of Jewish itjihad, not unlike any other form of religious cult." Jose Faur, *In the Shadow of History: Jews and Conversos at the Dawn of Modernity* (New York: SUNY, 1992), 13.

[22] His Commentary to Exodus 20:3 – Pirush ha-Ramban, Volume 1, p. 393 refers to the "science of magic and divination" as does his comments on Genesis 4:22 where he references "books on the use of demons." In addition, he was in contact with "masters of demons" with whom he had sought "clarification" from. See Torat Hashem Temima, pp.146, 149. Jose Faur, *In the Shadow of History: Jews and Conversos at the Dawn of Modernity* (New York: SUNY, 1992), 223.

Maimonidean view by attacking "those who pretend to be wise and emulate the Greek (i.e., Aristotle). Rabbi Moses ben Nachman was also an ardent believer in chirognomy and chiromancy, which he described as "ancient and authentic sciences."[23] Rabbi Moses ben Nachman stated:

> "This would be known with spirits through the science of necromancy (hokhmat ha-negromansia), and it also could be known to the minds through the clues of the Tora, to those who understand their secrets. And I cannot explain [further], because we would have to shut up the mouth of those who pretend to be wise about nature, emulating the Greek [i.e., Aristotle], who rejected everything that he could not perceive with the senses. And haughtily, he and his evil disciples thought that everything that he did not grasp with his reason is untrue."[24]

Nachmanides also saw Moses as an outstanding master of witchcraft and necromancy. Regarding Moses, Nachmanides wrote, "higher than all that, was that he knew all types of witchcraft, and from there he would ascend to the spheres, to the heavens and their hosts." King Solomon, too was regarded as an expert in sorcery, which was the wisdom of Egypt.[25] Nachmanides also believed in astrology and thought it wrong to contradict what astrological signs purportedly revealed. Jewish law, articulated in Maimonides' *Mishneh Torah*, was evident in the prohibition against astrology. Nachmanides also adhered to the belief in astrological medicine. These practices involved the use of

---

[23] Moses Lazar and Stephen Haliczer, Eds. *The Jews of Spain and the Expulsion of 1492* (Lancaster: Labyrinthos, 1997), 52.

[24] Keter ha-Torah, ed. R. Joseph Hasid (Jerusalem, 1970), vol. 3, 122b cited in Jose Faur, *In the Shadow of History: Jews and Conversos at the Dawn of Modernity* (New York: SUNY, 1992), 223.

[25] Moses Lazar and Stephen Haliczer, Eds. *The Jews of Spain and the Expulsion of 1492* (Lancaster: Labyrinthos, 1997), 52.

astrological images to treat specific ailments. Such views were in opposition to the position of Rabbi Abraham ibn Ezra and Rabbi Moses ben Maimon. The former went as far as to label the construction of such symbols as a transgression of the third commandment.[26]

For Faur, Nachmanides' views do not reflect anti-rationalistic sentiments seeking to affirm Jewish authority against non-Jewish cultural influences. It was instead distinct cultural patterns set in opposition to each other.[27] A significant shift in the community's philosophy and leadership was one of several critical factors transforming the Iberian Peninsula's Jewish community into a significantly weaker and more divided one. Also, the incorporation of demonology as a critical point of Kabbalistic theology oriented Judaism towards the elements that Christian thought considered fundamental to its theological makeup. As Faur notes:

> "What was truly revolutionary of the new ideology, from the point of view of Rabbinic tradition, was not the recognition of magic and demonology, but that these deviations were elevated to a dogma, indispensable for salvation."[28]

Christian Influences on Jewish Theology

The transformation in Jewish theology towards an anti-rationalistic trend was not the only element that surfaced to reshape the Jewish community's orientation radically. The influence of mystical traditions would introduce ideas that can only reveal new influences among Spanish Jewry. As previously noted, Rabbi

---

[26] Ibid., 53.
[27] Jose Faur, *In the Shadow of History: Jews and Conversos at the Dawn of Modernity* (New York: SUNY, 1992), 14.
[28] Moses Lazar and Stephen Haliczer, Eds. *The Jews of Spain and the Expulsion of 1492* (Lancaster: Labyrinthos, 1997), 51.

Solomon ben Aderet, who was a highly respected leader of the 13th and early 14th century, issued a ban against the Maimonidean support in Barcelona.

Combating the Maimonidean tradition, Rabbi Solomon ben Aderet defended "the true mystical traditions which are in the hands of the sages of Israel." Unintentionally, Rabbi Solomon ben Aderet cited ideas favorably from Ashkenazic mystical circles, which resembled Christian trinitarianism.

The martyrdom of St. Alban, from a 13th-century manuscript

The idea was intended to illuminate the ostensible mystery found in the opening prayer of the *Amidah* known as the *Avot*. The opening segment of the prayer reads, "the God of Abraham, the God of Isaac, and the God of Jacob" is compared to the expression "the God of the heavens and the earth." The mystical interpretation of the first phrase focused on the blessing's opening word, *Baruch* consisting of three Hebrew consonants *Bet*, *Resh*, and *Chaf Sofit*. According to the mystical interpretation, the three letters which constitute the word *Baruch* could be rearranged into various combinations. These rearrangements included *R-Ch-B*, which rendered the word "mounted." Another combination was *B-Ch-R*, meaning "firstborn." Another grouping could be the *Ch-R-B*, which could be translated as "Cherub."

The mystical tradition commented on the first permutation, *R-Ch-B*. It posited that it stood for God and "Provident and Savior." The second permutation, *B-Ch-R*, stood for God's dominion and greatness. *Ch-R-B* represented the understanding to which one a person should cleave. These three ideas were one, *B-Ch-R*. These ideas, Faur contended, could not despite the best intentions of Aderet, but be associated with the Christian doctrine of the Trinity. The Christian conceptions of the Father, Son, and Holy Spirit were "logical" connections to the idea of *Baruch*. While there may have been other arguments for doing so, Jewish apostates were appealing to the opening section of the Amidah as illustrating the mystery of the Trinity. Most surprising was the spread of Ashkenazic mystical traditions in Spain. According to Rabbi Solomon ibn Verga, Christians were being used by Christians to define the Trinity as reflective as wholly consistent with monotheism. The argument would continue to be interpreted as reflecting the Trinity's mystery through the end of the fifteenth century in and outside of the Iberian Peninsula through the seventeenth century.[29]

> "The Trinity is not polytheism but simple monotheism to those who understand. And I saw three men from the Ashkenazic sages, and I learned from them in the books of mysticism, and I saw how from there, it becomes evident how the Trinity is monotheism. And according to these words, I asked them [the Jews]: Who are then better, you or your forefathers?"[30]

The problem with the spread of these mystical traditions was not lost on Jewish apologists, particularly with the sefirotic imagery spread in Kabbalistic circles. When confronted with Trinitarian arguments, one Maimonidean adherent stated:

---

[29] Jose Faur, *In the Shadow of History: Jews and Conversos at the Dawn of Modernity* (New York: SUNY, 1992), 14.

[30] Rabbi Solomon ibn Verga, Shebet Yehuda, VII, p.37 cited in Jose Faur, *In the Shadow of History: Jews and Conversos at the Dawn of Modernity* (New York: SUNY, 1992), 15.

"[Whereas] the Christians believe in the Trinity, the mystics believe in the Ten (sefirot)."

Faur points out the critique of Nachmanides orientation towards Kabbalistic thought as Rabbi Nissim Gerondi noted regarding the former:

"the Ramban [= Rabbi Moses Ben Nachman] became very excessively committed to believing in topics of that mysticism."[31]

It is impossible to know what the average Jew would have comprehended regarding the mystical traditions mentioned. To those uninitiated to the intricacies of theology, it could, however, have very quickly marred the lines between Judaism and Christianity, particularly in a crisis. Maimonides' *Iggeret ha-Shamad* assumed a monotheistic view of Islam. While Christianity was harder to designate as purely monotheistic, the views above were possibly sufficient to stir the argument towards accepting that plausibility or at least diminishing the degree of theological revision a Jew may have felt when faced with coerced conversion as a means to survive.

Shifting Models of Jewish Leadership

The shift towards Kabbalah as a critical paradigm of thought among Spanish Jews was coupled with a gradual shift in rabbinic leadership by emigration and a radical change in the Jewish scholarship in the Talmudic academies. The notion of a *talmid chacham* as a master of halakhah was replaced by increasing numbers of rabbinic students dedicated to a dialectical method referred to as *pilpul*.

---

[31] Rabbi Isaac Bar Sheshet, *Teshubot ha-Ribash*, no. 157 cited in Jose Faur, *In the Shadow of History: Jews and Conversos at the Dawn of Modernity* (New York: SUNY, 1992), 15.

The change in emphasis led to a decline in the scholarship of rabbinic circles. This, coupled with the shift towards religious fervor at the expense of ethics and morality, eroded the Jewish community's leadership when it was most needed.[32] Rabbi Solomon Al'ami, in his *Iggeret Mouser,* notes the following:

> "Some of our recent sages lost their way in the wilderness! They erred [even with] the most obvious! Because they hate and are jealous of each other, and put up for sale the Torah for presents. The goal of their curriculum is to know how to read [the Torah] meticulously and expand their own innovations. The study of the Talmud and other works [also is wanting] because they are concerned with every minute detail of the law and the different views and opinions [not with its substance]. They thrust aside the humility of the virtuous, temperance, and holiness. What [-one rabbi] instructs the other darkens; what [one rabbi permits the other prohibits. Through their quarrels, the law had become two!"[33]

Benzion Netanyahu interpreting Alami suggests that "caustic, truth-evading, and self-seeking rabbinic scholars and…unprincipled Jewish courtiers…" were secondary causes of subsequent mass conversions.[34]

---

[32] Jose Faur, *In the Shadow of History: Jews and Conversos at the Dawn of Modernity* (New York: SUNY, 1992), 19, 21.

[33] Rabbi Solomon Al'Ami, *Iggeret Musar,* A.A. Haberman, ed. (Jerusalem, 1946), 40-41.

[34] Allan Harris Cutler and Helen Elmquist Cutler, *The Jews as Ally of the Muslim: Medieval Roots of Anti-Semitism* (Notre Dame: University of Notre Dame, 1986), 253.

Conclusions

The violence that Iberian Jews faced in the medieval period was real. Their response to this violence was filtered through their religious, cultural, and social environment. Some Iberian Jews chose martyrdom as the highest reflection of devotion to the Jewish faith. Other Jews, perhaps understanding the complexity of Jewish religious thought on the matter and the Iberian Peninsula's past Jewish experience, chose dissimulation to survive.

There is no question that other Jews converted to Christianity for reasons other than the direct threat of violence. Many individuals experienced a financial disaster as economic opportunities for Jews lessened throughout the 15th century. Faced with financial ruin or even starvation, many Jews opted for conversion.

Others saw more significant opportunities as Christians. Their existing religious commitment did not provide a primary motivation for many. Conversion to Christianity opened social and economic prospects.

Others did not necessarily see the stark differences between Judaism and Christianity. Changing theological approaches in Jewish thought may have made Christian ideas more acceptable, especially when faced with other factors. There were possible elements of all these factors that contributed to many Iberian Jews' decision to convert.

Bibliography

Abrera, Anna Ysabel D. *The Tribunal of Zaragoza and Crypto-Judaism, 1484-1515.* Turnhout, Belgium: Brepols, 2008.

Adler, Cyrus, and Isidore Singer. "Inquisition." Jewish Encyclopedia. 1906. Accessed June 9, 2015. http://www.jewishencyclopedia.com/articles/8122-inquisition.

Adler, Cyrus, and Isidore Singer. "Apostasy and Apostates from Judaism." Jewish Encyclopedia. 1906. Accessed June 9, 2015. http://www.jewishencyclopedia.com/articles/1654-apostasy-and-apostates-from-judaism.

"Al-Taqiyya, Dissimulation Part 1." Al Islam. Accessed June 2, 2015. http://www.al-islam.org/shiite-encyclopedia-ahlul-bayt-dilp-team/al-taqiyya-dissimulation-part-1.

Albert, Bat-Sheva. "Isidore of Seville: His Attitude Towards Judaism and His Impact on Early Medieval Canon Law." *The Jewish Quarterly Review* 80, no. 3-4 (1990): 207-20.

Alfassa, Shelomo. *The Sephardic 'Anousim': The Forcibly Converted Jews of Spain and Portugal.* New York: ISLC, 2010.

Alpert, Michael. *Crypto-judaism and the Spanish Inquisition.* Basingstoke, Hampshire: Palgrave, 2001.

Alter, Alexandra. "'Secret Jews' of the Spanish Inquisition." Derkeiler. August 6, 2005. Accessed March 30, 2015. http://newsgroups.derkeiler.com/Archive/Soc/soc.culture.cuba/2005-08/msg00977.html.

Altmann, Alexander. "Eternality of Punishment: A Theological Controversy within the Amsterdam Rabbinate in the Thirties of the Seventeenth Century." *Proceedings of the American Academy for Jewish Research* 40 (1972): 1-88.

Amital, Yehuda. "A Torah Perspective on the Status of Secular Jews Today." The Israel Koschitzky Virtual Beit Midrash. Accessed January 13, 2015. http://etzion.org.il/vbm/english/alei/2-2chilo.htm.

Amran, Rica. "Judíos Y Conversos En Las Crónicas De Los Reyes De Castilla (desde Finales Del Siglo XIV Hasta La Expulsión)." *Espacio, Tiempo Y Forma* Serie III, no. 9 (1996): 257-76.

Antine, Nissan. "Responsa Relating to the Conversos." Lecture, from Beth Sholom and Talmud Torah, Potomac, January 1, 2010.

Antonio Escudero, José. "Luis Vives Y La Inquisicion." *Revista De La Inquisición : Intolerancia Y Derechos Humanos* 13 (2009): 11-24.

Assis, Yom Tov. "The Jews of the Maghreb and Sepharad: A Case Study of Inter-communal Cultural Relations through the Ages." *El Prezente* 2 (2008): 11-30.

Baer, Yitzhak. *A History of the Jews in Christian Spain*. Vol. II. Philadelphia: Jewish Publication Society of America, 1961.

Barnai, Jacob. "Christian Messianism and the Portuguese Marranos: The Emergence of Sabbateanism in Smyrna." *Jew History Jewish History* 7, no. 2 (1993): 119-26.

Baron, Salo W. *A Social and Religious History of the Jews*. Vol. IV. Philadelphia: Jewish Publication Society, 1957.

Baron, Salo W. *A Social and Religious History of the Jews*. Vol. IX. New York: Columbia University Press, 1965.

Baron, Salo W. *A Social and Religious History of the Jews*. Vol. X. Philadelphia: Jewish Publication Society, 1965.

Baron, Salo W. *A Social and Religious History of the Jews*. Vol. XI. Philadelphia: Jewish Publication Society, 1967.

Baron, Salo W. *A Social and Religious History of the Jews*. Vol. XIII. Philadelphia: Jewish Publication Society, 1969.

Baxter Wolf, Kenneth. "Sentencia-Estatuto De Toledo, 1449." Texts in Translation. 2008. Accessed June 2, 2015. https://sites.google.com/site/canilup/toledo1449.

Beinart, Haim, and Yael Guiladi. *Conversos on Trial: The Inquisition in Ciudad Real*. Jerusalem: Magnes Press, Hebrew University, 1981.

Beinart, Haim. *The Expulsion of the Jews from Spain*. Oxford: Littman Library of Jewish Civilization, 2002.

Ben-Sasson, Menahem. "On the Jewish Identity of Forced Converts: A Study of Forced Conversion in the Almohade Period." *Pe'amim* 42 (1990): 16-37.

Ben-Shalom, Ram. "Between Official and Private Dispute: The Case of Christian Spain and Provence in the Late Middle Ages." *AJS Review* 27, no. 1, 23-71.

Ben-Shalom, Ram. "The Converso as Subversive: Jewish Traditions or Christian Libel?" *Journal of Jewish Studies* 50, no. 2 (1999): 259-83.

Ben-Shalom, Ram. "The Typology of the Converso in Isaac Abravanel's Biblical Exegesis." *Jew History Jewish History* 23, no. 3 (2009): 281-92.

Ben-Ur, Aviva. "Fakelore" or Historically Overlooked Sub-Ethnic Group?" HNet Humanities and Social Sciences Online. 2010. Accessed June 9, 2015. http://www.h-net.org/reviews/showrev.php?id=29438.

Benveniste, Arthur. "Finding Our Lost Brothers and Sisters: The Crypto-Jews of Brazil." *Western States Jewish History* 29, no. 3 (1997): 103-09.

Benveniste, Henriette-Rika. "On the Language of Conversion: Visigothic Spain Revisited." *Historein* 6 (2006): 72-87.

Berenbaum, Michael, and Fred Skolnik eds. "Isaac Ben Sheshet Perfet." *Encyclopedia Judaica*. 2nd ed. Vol. 10. Detroit: Macmillan, 2007.

Bermúdez Vázquez, Manuel. "Intuiciones De Criptojudaísmo En El "Quod Nihil Scitur" De Francisco Sánchez." *Revista Internacional De Filosofía* 13 (2008): 285-94.

Bermúdez Vázquez, Manuel. "La Influencia Del Pensamiento Judeo-cristiano En Michel De Montaigne, Giordano Bruno Y Francisco Sánchez." *Ámbitos* 23 (2010): 19-27.
Bodian, Miriam. "Hebrews of the Portuguese Nation: The Ambiguous Boundaries of Self-Definition." *Jewish Social Studies* 15, no. 1 (2008): 66-80.
Bodian, Miriam. *Hebrews of the Portuguese Nation: Conversos and Community in Early Modern Amsterdam*. Bloomington: Indiana University Press, 1997.
"B'nei Anusim." Be'chol Lashon. Accessed June 9, 2015. http://www.bechollashon.org/projects/spanish/anusim.php.
Carpenter, Dwayne. "From Al-Burak to Alboraycos: The Art of Transformation on the Eve of the Expulsion." In *Jews and Conversos at the Time of the Expulsion*. Jerusalem: Zalman Shazar for Jewish History, 1999.
Carvajal, Luis De, and Seymour B. Liebman. *The Enlightened; the Writings of Luis De Carvajal, El Mozo*. Coral Gables, Fla.: University of Miami Press, 1967.
Carvalho, Joaquim. *Religion and Power in Europe: Conflict and Convergence*. Pisa: PLUS-Pisa University Press, 2007.
Chazan, Robert. *European Jewry and the First Crusade*. Berkeley: University of California Press, 1987.
Cohen, Jeremy. "Between Martyrdom and Apostasy: Doubt and Self-definition in Twelfth-century Ashkenaz." *Journal of Medieval and Early Modern Studies* 29, no. 3 (1999): 431-71.
Cohen, Mark R. *Under Crescent and Cross: The Jews in the Middle Ages*. Princeton, N.J.: Princeton University Press, 1994.
Cohen, Shaye J. D. *The Beginnings of Jewishness Boundaries, Varieties, Uncertainties*. Berkeley: University of California Press, 1999.
"Conversos & Crypto-Jews." City of Albuquerque. Accessed June 9, 2015. http://www.cabq.gov/humanrights/public-information-and-education/diversity-booklets/jewish-american-heritage/conversos-crypto-jews.
"Crypto-Jews." Am I Jewish? Accessed March 25, 2015. http://www.amijewish.info/w/crypto-jews/.
Cutler, Allan Harris, and Helen Elmquist Cutler. *The Jew as Ally of the Muslim: Medieval Roots of Anti-Semitism*. Notre Dame, Ind.: University of Notre Dame Press, 1986.
Davidson, Herbert A. *Moses Maimonides: The Man and His Works*. Oxford: Oxford University Press, 2005.
Dorff, Elliot N., and Arthur I. Rosett. *A Living Tree the Roots and Growth of Jewish Law*. Albany, N.Y.: the State University of New York Press, 1988.
Faur, Jose. *In the Shadow of History Jews and Conversos at the Dawn of Modernity*. Albany, N.Y.: the State University of New York Press, 1992.
Faur, José. "Four Classes of Conversos." *Revue Des Études Juives* 149, no. 1-2 (1990): 113-24.
Faur, José. "Anti-Maimonidean Demons." *Review of Rabbinic Judaism* 6 (2003): 3-52.

Ferry, Barbara, and Debbie Nathan. "Mistaken Identity? The Case of New Mexico's "Hidden Jews." The Atlantic. December 1, 2000. Accessed April 1, 2015. http://www.theatlantic.com/magazine/archive/2000/12/mistaken-identity-the-case-of-new-mexicos-hidden-jews/378454/ I.

Ferziger, Adam S. "Between 'Ashkenazi' and Sepharad: An Early Modern German Rabbinic Response to Religious Pluralism in the Spanish-Portuguese Community." *Studia Rosenthaliana* 35, no. 1 (2001): 7-22.

Fishman, Talya. "The Jewishness of the Conversos." Lecture, Early Modern Workshop: Jewish History Resources, January 1, 2004.

Foer, Paul, and Chananette Pascal Cohen. "For Hispanic 'Crypto-Jews,' Lawsuits May Follow Religious Rediscovery." JNS. October 29, 2012. Accessed March 25, 2015. http://www.jns.org/latest-articles/2012/10/29/for-hispanic-crypto-jews-lawsuits-may-follow-religious-redis.html#.VXdW0dLBzGd.

Fram, Edward. "Perception and Reception of Repentant Apostates in Medieval Ashkenaz and Premodern Poland." *AJS Review* 21, no. 2 (1996): 299-339.

Frank, Daniel, and Matt Goldfish. *Rabbinic Culture and Its Critics: Jewish Authority, Dissent, and Heresy in the Medieval and Early Modern Times*. Detroit: Wayne State University, 2007.

Friedenwald, Harry. "Montaigne's Relation to Judaism and the Jews." *The Jewish Quarterly Review* 31, no. 2 (1940): 141-48.

Furst, Rachel. "Captivity, Conversion, and Communal Identity: Sexual Angst and Religious Crisis in Frankfurt, 1241." *Jew History Jewish History* 22, no. 1-2 (2008): 179-221.

Gampel, Benjamin R. "The 'Identity' of Sephardim of Medieval Christian Iberia." *Jewish Social Studies* 8, no. 2/3 (2002): 133-38.

Gerber, Jane S. *The Jews of Spain*. New York: The Free Press, 1992.

Gilman, Stephen. *The Spain of Fernando De Rojas; the Intellectual and Social Landscape of La Celestina*. Princeton, N.J.: Princeton University Press, 1972.

Gitlitz, David M. *Secrecy and Deceit: The Religion of the Crypto-Jews*. Philadelphia: Jewish Publication Society, 1996.

Goldish, Matt. *The Sabbatean Prophets*. Cambridge, Mass.: Harvard University Press, 2004.

Golinkin, David. "How Can Apostates Such as the Falash Mura Return to Judaism?" *Responsa in a Moment* 1, no. 5, (2007). Accessed June 9, 2015. http://www.schechter.edu/responsa.aspx?ID=30.

Gomez-Hortiguela Amillo, Angel. "La Vida Sine Querella De Juan Luis Vives." *EHumanista* 26 (2014): 345-56.

Grayzel, Solomon. "The Beginnings of Exclusion." *The Jewish Quarterly Review* 61, no. 1 (1970): 15-26.

Grayzel, Solomon. *The Church and the Jews in the XIIIth Century*. New York: Hermon, 1966.

Green, Simcha. "Welcoming Anusim Back Into The Family." The Jewish Press. August 22, 2012. Accessed March 25, 2015. http://www.jewishpress.com/indepth/opinions/welcoming-anusim-back-into-the-family/2010/12/08/0/?print.

Green, Toby. *The Reign of Fear*. London: Macmillan: 2007.

Guerson, Alexandra. "Seeking Remission: Jewish Conversion in the Crown of Aragon, C.1378–1391." *Jewish History* 24, no. 1 (2010): 33-52.

Gutwirth, Eleazar. "The Jews in 15th Century Castilian Chronicles." *The Jewish Quarterly Review* 74, no. 4 (1984): 379-96.

Halevy, Schulamith C., and Nachum Dershowitz. "Obscure Practices among New World Anusim." *Proceedings of the Conferencia Internacional De Investigacion De La Asociacion Latinoamericana De Estudios Judaicos*, 1995. Accessed June 9, 2015.

Haliczer, Stephen. "Conversos Y Judíos En Tiempos De La Expulsión : Un Análisis Crítico De Investigación Y Análisis." *Revistas Espacio, Tiempo Y Forma* Serie III (1993): 287-300.

"Jewish History Sourcebook: The Jews of Spain and the Visigothic Code, 654-681 CE." Fordham University. 1998. Accessed June 2, 2015. http://legacy.fordham.edu/halsall/jewish/jews-visigothic1.asp.

Halperin, David J. trans. Abraham Miguel Cardozo; Selected Writings. New York: Paulist Press, 2001.

Hayim Sofer, Yitshaq BenTsvi Ben Naftali. *Sefer Shu " T Ha-Radbaz Mi-Ktav Yad*. Benei Brak, 1975.

Hershman, A.M. *Rabbi Isaac Bar Sheshet Perfet and His Times*. New York, N.Y.: Jewish Theological Seminary, 1943.

Hinojosa Montalvo, José. "Los Judíos En La España Medieval: De La Tolerancia a La Expulsión." In *Los Marginados En El Mundo Medieval Y Moderno.*, 25-41. Almería: Instituto De Estudios Almerienses, 1998.

Hochbaum, Jerry. "Who Is a Jew: A Sociological Perspective." *Tradition* 13/14, no. 4/1 (1973): 35-41.

Hopstein, Avner. "The Crypto-Jews of Brazil." Y Net News. October 26, 2006. Accessed March 31, 2015. http://www.ynetnews.com/articles/0,7340,L-3319972,00.html.

Hordes, Stanley M. *To the End of the Earth: A History of the Crypto-Jews of New Mexico*. New York: Columbia University Press, 2005.

Idel, Moshe. *Messianic Mystics*. New Haven: Yale University Press, 1998.

Ingram, Kevin. *Secret Lives, Public Lies the Conversos and Socio-religious Nonconformism in the Spanish Golden Age*. San Diego, California: UC San Diego Electronic Theses and Dissertations, 2006.

Ingram, Kevin, ed. *The Conversos and Moriscos in Late Medieval Spain and beyond*. Vol. 2. Leiden: Brill, 2012.

Israel, Jonathan. "Sephardic Immigration into the Dutch Republic, 1595-1672." *Studia Rosenthaliana* 23 (1989): 45-53.

Israel, Jonathan. "Spain and the Dutch Sephardim, 1609-1660." *Studia Rosenthaliana* 12, no. 1/2 (1978): 1-61.

Jacobs, Louis. "Attitudes towards Christianity in the Halakhah." Louis Jacobs. 2005. Accessed June 1, 2015. http://louisjacobs.org/articles/attitudes-towards-christianity-in-the-halakhah/?highlight=Attitudes towards Christianity.

Jocz, Jakob. *The Jewish People and Jesus Christ; a Study in the Relationship between the Jewish People and Jesus Christ.* London: S.P.C.K., 1949.

JOSPIC -J Staff "A List of 134 Books Containing Marrano, Converso, Crypto-Jew, Secret Jew, Hidden Jew, New Christian, or Anusim in the Title or Subtitle: Changes in Usage Over 86 Years." *Journal of Spanish, Portuguese, and Italian Crypto-Jews*, 2011, 149-55.

Juster, J. *Les Juifs Dans L'Empire Romain*. Vol. II. Paris: P. Geunther, 1914.

Kaplan, Yosef. "The Portuguese Jews in Amsterdam: From Forced Conversion to a Return to Judaism." *Studia Rosenthaliana* 15, no. 1 (1981): 37-51.

Kaplan, Yosef. "The Jewish Profile of the Spanish-Portuguese Community of London during the Seventeenth Century." *Judaism* 41, no. 3 (1992): 229-40.

Kaplan, Yosef. "Wayward New Christians and Stubborn New Jews: The Shaping of a Jewish Identity." *Jewish History* 8, no. 1-2 (1994): 27-41.

Katz, Jacob. *Exclusiveness and Tolerance; Studies in Jewish-gentile Relations in Medieval and Modern Times.* West Orange: Behrman House, 1961.

Katz, Jacob. *Halakhah Ve-Qabbalah.* Jerusalem: Magnes Press, 1984.

Katz, Solomon. *The Jews in the Visigothic and Frankish Kingdoms of Spain and Gaul.* New York: Kraus, 1970.

Kedourie, Elie. *Spain and the Jews: The Sephardi Experience: 1492 and after.* London: Thames and Hudson, 1992.

Kelly, David. "DNA Clears the Fog Over Latino Links to Judaism in New Mexico." Los Angeles Times. December 5, 2004. Accessed March 25, 2015. http://articles.latimes.com/2004/dec/05/nation/na-heritage5.

Krow-Lucal, Martha G. "Marginalizing History: Observations on the Origins of the Inquisition in Fifteenth-century Spain by B. Netanyahu." *Judaism*, 1997, 47-62.

Kunin, David A. "Welcoming Back the Anusim: A Halakhic Teshuvah." Sephardim Hope. July 9, 2009. Accessed June 10, 2015. http://sephardim-hope.net/index.php?view=article&catid=36:articles&id=62:welcoming-back-the-anusim-a-halakhic-teshuvah&format=pdf&option=com_content&Itemid=69.

Lavender, Abraham D. "The Secret Jews (Neofiti) of Sicily: Religious and Social Status Before and After the Inquisition." *Journal of Spanish, Portuguese, and Italian Crypto-Jews* 3 (2011): 119-33.

Lawrance, Jeremy. "Alegoría Y Apocalipsis En "El Alboraique"" *Revista De Poética Medieval* 11 (2003): 11-39.

Lazar, Moshe. *The Jews of Spain and the Expulsion of 1492.* Lancaster, Calif.: Labyrinthos, 1997.

Lea, Henry Charles. "Ferrand Martinez and the Massacres of 1391." *The American Historical Review* 1, no. 2 (1896): 209-19.

Leibman, Seymour. *The Jews in New Spain*. Miami: University of Miami, 1970.
Lent, Dani. "Analysis of the Israeli High Courts: Jewish Apostates and the Law of Return." Kol Hamevaser. 2010. Accessed June 1, 2015. http://www.kolhamevaser.com/2010/09/analysis-of-the-israeli-high-court-jewish-apostates-and-the-law-of-return/.
Lewis, Bernard. *The Jews of Islam*. Princeton, N.J.: Princeton University Press, 1984.
Lichenstein, Aharon. *Brother Daniel and Jewish Fraternity, Leaves of Faith: The World of Jewish Living*. Jersey City: Ktav, 2004.
Lieberman, Julia R. "Sermons and the Construct of a Jewish Identity: The Hamburg Sephardic Community in the 1620s." *Jewish Studies Quarterly* 10, no. 1 (2003): 49-72.
Liebman, Seymour B. *The Jews in New Spain; Faith, Flame, and the Inquisition*, Coral Gables, Fla.: University of Miami Press, 1970.
Liebman, Seymour B. *New World Jewry, 1493-1825: Requiem for the Forgotten*. New York: Ktav Pub. House, 1982.
Linder, Amnon. *The Jews in Roman Imperial Legislation*. Detroit, Mich.: Wayne State University Press, 1987.
Lindo, E.H. *The Jews of Spain and Portugal*. London: Longman, Brown, Green, & Longmans, 1848.
Lipshiz, Cnaan. "Secret No More." Shavei Israel. November 9, 2009. Accessed March 25, 2015. http://www.shavei.org/communities/bnei_anousim/articles-bnei_anousim/secret-no-more/?lang=en.
Llobet Portella, Josep Maria. "Los Conversos Según La Documentación Local De Cervera (1338-1501)." *Revista De La Facultad De Geografía E Historia* 4 (1989): 335-49.
Maimonides, Moses, and Abraham S. Halkin. *Crisis and Leadership: Epistles of Maimonides*. Philadelphia: Jewish Publication Society of America, 1985.
Marcus, Jacob Rader. *The Jew in the Medieval World: A Source Book, 315-1791*. Cincinnati: Union of American Hebrew Congregations, 1938.
Margaliot, Reuben. *Sefer Ḥasidim*. Jerusalem: Mosad Ha-Rav Ḳook, 1956.
"Marranos, Conversos & New Christians." Jewish Virtual Library. Accessed June 1, 2015. https://www.jewishvirtuallibrary.org/jsource/Judaism/Marranos.html.
Martin, J. J. "Marranos and Nicodemites in Sixteenth-Century Venice." *Journal of Medieval and Early Modern Studies* 41, no. 3 (2011): 577-99.
Mentzer, Raymond A. "Marranos of Southern France in the Early Sixteenth Century." *The Jewish Quarterly Review* 72, no. 4 (1982): 303-11.
Metzger, David, ed. *Sheelot U-Teshuvot Le-rabbenu Ha-gadol Marana Ve-rabbana Ha-rav Yiẓḥak Bar Sheshet*. Jerusalem: Makhon Or HaMizrah, 1993.
Meyers, Charles, and Norman Simms eds. *Troubled Souls: Conversos, Crypto-Jews, and Other Confused Jewish Intellectuals from the Fourteenth through the Eighteenth Century*. Hamilton: Outrigger Publishers, 2001.
Meyerson, Mark D. "Aragonese and Catalan Jewish Converts at the Time of the Expulsion." *Jewish History*, 1992, 131-49.

Meyerson, Mark D. *A Jewish Renaissance in Fifteenth-century Spain*. Princeton: Princeton University Press, 2004.
Montalvo, Jose. *The Jews of the Kingdom of Valencia: From Persecution to Expulsion, 1391-1492*. Jerusalem: Magnes Press, Hebrew University, 1993.
Nelson, Zalman. "Is a Jew Who Converts Still Jewish?" Chabad. Accessed June 2, 2015. http://www.chabad.org/library/article_cdo/aid/1269075/jewish/Is-a-Jew-Who-Converts-Still-Jewish.htm.
Netanyahu, B. "Americo Castro and His View of the Origins of the Pureza De Sangre." *Proceedings of the American Academy for Jewish Research* 46/47, no. Jubilee Volume (1928-29 / 1978-79) (1979): 397-457.
Netanyahu, B. *The Origins of the Inquisition in Fifteenth-Century Spain*. New York: Random House, 1995.
Netanyahu, B. *The Marranos of Spain: From the Late 14th to the Early 16th Century, According to Contemporary Hebrew Sources*. 3rd ed. Ithaca, N.Y.: Cornell University Press, 1999.
Nirenberg, David. "Conversion, Sex, And Segregation: Jews And Christians In Medieval Spain." *The American Historical Review* 107, no. 4 (2002): 1065-093.
Nirenberg, David. *Anti-Judaism: The Western Tradition*. New York: W. W. Norton &, 2013.
Nissimi, Hilda. "Religious Conversion, Covert Defiance and Social Identity: A Comparative View." *Numen* 51, no. 4 (2004): 367-406.
"Obituary Samuel Lerer, an American Rabbi Who Converted Mexicans, Dies at 89." Jewish Telegraph Agency. February 9, 2004. Accessed March 25, 2015. http://www.jta.org/2004/02/09/archive/obituary-samuel-lerer-an-american-rabbi-who-converted-mexicans-dies-at-89.
Oeltjen, Natalie. *Crisis and Regeneration: The Conversos of Majorca, 1391-1416*. Toronto: University of Toronto, 2012.
Orme, Wyatt. "Crypto-Jews' In the Southwest Find Faith in a Shrouded Legacy." Code Switch Frontiers of Race, Culture, and Ethnicity. February 19, 2014. Accessed March 25, 2015. http://www.npr.org/sections/codeswitch/2014/02/19/275862633/crypto-jews-in-the-southwest-find-faith-in-a-shrouded-legacy.
Parello, Vincent. "La Apologética Antijudía De Juan Luis Vives (1543)." *Melanges De La Casa De Velazquez* 38, no. 2 (2008): 171-87.
Perez, Joseph, and Lysa Hochroth. *History of a Tragedy: The Expulsion of the Jews from Spain*. Chicago: University of Illinois Press, 1993.
Perlmann, Moshe. "Apostasy." Jewish Virtual Library. 2008. Accessed June 2, 2015. http://www.jewishvirtuallibrary.org/jsource/judaica/ejud_0002_0002_0_01188.html.
Popkin, Richard H. *The History of Scepticism from Erasmus to Spinoza*. Rev. and Expanded ed. Berkeley: University of California Press, 1979.
"Portugal." Jewish Virtual Library, accessed on July 28, 2015, http://www.jewishvirtuallibrary.org/jsource/vjw/Portugal.html

Quesada Morillas, Yolanda. "La Expulsion De Los Judios Andaluces a Finales Del Siglo XV Y Su Prohibicion De Pase a Indias." *Actas Del I Congreso Internacional Sobre Migraciones En Andalucia*, 2011, 2099-106.

Rábade Obrado, María Del Pilar. "La Instrucción Cristiana De Los Conversos En La Castilla Del Siglo XV." *En La España Medieval* 22 (1999): 369-93.

Raphael, Amia. "Goldsmiths and Silversmiths." Jewish Virtual Library, accessed on July 31, 2015. http://www.jewishvirtuallibrary.org/jsource/judaica/ejud_0002_0007_0_07579.html.

Rosenblatt, Eli. "Picturing Today's Conversos." The Forward. April 1, 2008. Accessed March 25, 2015. http://forward.com/culture/13079/picturing-today-s-conversos-01595/.

Rosenbloom, Noah H. "Menasseh Ben Israel and the Eternality of Punishment Issue." *Proceedings of the American Academy for Jewish Research* 60 (1994): 241-62.

Rosenstock, Bruce. "Abraham Miguel Cardoso's Messianism: A Reappraisal." *AJS Review* 23, no. 1 (1998): 63-104.

Ross, Theodore. "Shalom on the Range: In Search of the American Crypto-Jew." Harpers. December 1, 2009. Accessed March 27, 2015. http://harpers.org/archive/2009/12/shalom-on-the-range/.

Roth, Cecil. *A History of the Marranos*. Philadelphia: Jewish Publication Society of America, 1947.

Roth, Cecil. *The Spanish Inquisition*. New York: WW. Norton and Company, 1964.

Roth, Norman. "Anti-Converso Riots of the Fifteenth Century, Pulgar, and the Inquisition." *En la España Medieval* 15 (1992): 367-94.

Roth, Norman. *Jews, Visigoths, and Muslims in Medieval Spain: Cooperation and Conflict*. Leiden: E.J. Brill, 1994.

Roth, Norman. *Conversos, Inquisition, and the Expulsion of the Jews from Spain*. Madison, Wis.: University of Wisconsin Press, 1995.

Ruderman, David B. *Jewish Thought and Scientific Discovery in Early Modern Europe*. Detroit, Michigan: Wayne State University, 2001.

Sachar, Howard Morley. *Farewell España: The World of the Sephardim Remembered*. New York: Knopf, 1995.

Salomon, H.P. "New Light on the Portuguese Inquisition: The Second Reply to the Archbishop of Cranganor." *Studia Rosenthaliana* 5, no. 2 (1971): 178-86.

Sanchez, Francisco, and Douglas F.S. Thomson. *That Nothing Is Known*. Edited by Elaine Limbrick. Cambridge: Cambridge University Press, 1988.

Saperstein, Marc. "Christianity, Christians, and 'New Christians' in the Sermons of Saul Levi Morteira." *Hebrew Union College Annual* 70/71:329-84.

Saperstein, Marc. "Saul Levi Morteira's Treatise on the Immortality of the Soul." *Studia Rosenthaliana* 25, no. 2 (1991): 131-48.

Schiffman, Lawrence H. *Who Was a Jew?: Rabbinic and Halakhic Perspectives on the Jewish-Christian Schism*. Hoboken, N.J.: Ktav Pub. House, 1985.

Scholberg, Kenneth R. "Minorities in Medieval Castilian Literature." *Hispania* 37, no. 2 (1954): 203-09.
Scholem, Gershom. *The Messianic Idea in Judaism: And Other Essays on Jewish Spirituality.* New York: Schocken Books, 1972.
Selke, Angela. *Los Chuetas Y La Inquicision.* Madrid: Taurus, 1972.
Shatzmiller, Joseph. "Converts and Judaizers in the Early Fourteenth Century." *Harvard Theological Review* 74, no. 1 (1981): 63-77.
Sherwin, Byron L. *Faith Finding Meaning: A Theology of Judaism.* Oxford: Oxford University Press, 2009.
Singer, Isidore, and Cyrus Adler, eds. "Spain." *Jewish Encyclopedia.* 1906.
Spinoza, Benedictus De, and Dagobert D. Runes. *The Ethics Of Spinoza: The Road to Inner Freedom.* Secaucus: Citadel, 1976.
Stern, Sacha. *Jewish Identity in Early Rabbinic Writings.* New York: Brill, 1994.
Stillman, Norman A. *The Jews of Arab Lands: A History and Source Book.* Philadelphia: Jewish Publication Society of America, 1979.
Suarez Bilbao, Fernando. "Cristianos Contra Judios y Conversos." Lecture, from Universidad Rey Juan Carlos, Madrid, January 1, 2004.
Swetschinski, Daniel M. "Kinship and Commerce: The Foundations of Portuguese Jewish Life in Seventeenth-Century Holland." *Studia Rosenthaliana* 15, no. 1 (1981): 52-74.
Synan, Edward A. *The Popes and the Jews in the Middle Ages.* New York: Macmillan, 1965.
Szajkowski, Zosa. "Trade Relations of Marranos in France with the Iberian Peninsula in the Sixteenth and Seventeenth Centuries." *The Jewish Quarterly Review* 50, no. 1 (1959): 69-78.
Thornton, Stuart. "Hidden History: Rabbi Explains the Identity of the Crypto-Jews." National Geographic. Accessed March 25, 2015. http://www.nationalgeographic.com/hidden-history/.
Touger, Eliyahu. "Avodah Kochavim - Chapter Two." Chabad. Accessed June 9, 2015. http://www.chabad.org/library/article_cdo/aid/912360/jewish/Avodah-Kochavim-Chapter-Two.htm.
Touger, Eliyahu. "Ma'achalot Assurot - Chapter 17." Chabad. Accessed June 9, 2015. http://www.chabad.org/library/article_cdo/aid/968273/jewish/Maachalot-Assurot-Chapter-17.htm.
Touger, Eliyahu. "Gerushin - Chapter Three." Chabad. Accessed June 9, 2015. http://www.chabad.org/library/article_cdo/aid/957708/jewish/Gerushin-Chapter-Three.htm.
Touger, Eliyahu. "Yibbum VChalitzah - Chapter One." Chabad. Accessed June 9, 2015. http://www.chabad.org/library/article_cdo/aid/960619/jewish/Yibbum-vChalitzah-Chapter-One.htm.
Treatman, Ronit. "Queen Esther: Patron Saint of Crypto-Jews." The Times of Israel. March 16, 2014. Accessed April 2, 2015. http://www.timesofisrael.com/queen-esther-patron-saint-of-crypto-jews/.

Usque, Samuel, and Martin Cohen. *Consolations for the Tribulations of Israel (Consolacam as Tribulacoens De Israel)*. Philadelphia: Jewish Publication Society of America, 1977.

Utterback, Kristine T. " Conversi" Revert: Voluntary and Forced Return to Judaism in the Early Fourteenth Century." *Church History* 64, no. 1 (1995): 16-28.

Wakefield, Walter L. *Heresy, Crusade, and Inquisition in Southern France, 1100-1250*. Berkeley: University of California Press, 1974.

Wheelwright, Jeff. "The 'Secret Jews' of San Luis Valley." Smithsonian Magazine. 2008. Accessed March 25, 2015. http://www.smithsonianmag.com/science-nature/the-secret-jews-of-san-luis-valley-11765512/?no-ist.

Wildman, Sarah. "Mallorca's Jews Get Their Due: Spanish Island's Community Alive and Thriving." The Forward. April 13, 2012. Accessed March 27, 2015. http://forward.com/articles/154649/mallorcas-jews-get-their-due/?p=all#ixzz3TLpkmfSl.

Wiznitzer, Arnold. "Crypto-Jews in Mexico during the Sixteenth Century." *American Jewish Historical Quarterly* 51, no. 3 (1962): 168-214.

Yerushalmi, Yosef. "The Re-education of the Marranos in the Seventeenth Century." Scribd. 1980. Accessed June 2, 2015. http://www.scribd.com/doc/63071643/Re-Education-of-the-Marranos-by-Yosef-Yerushalmi#scribd.

Yerushalmi, Yosef Hayim. "The Inquisition and the Jews of France in the Time of Bernard Gui." *Harvard Theological Review* 63, no. 3 (1970): 317-76.

Yerushalmi, Yosef Hayim. *From Spanish Court to Italian Ghetto; Isaac Cardoso; a Study in Seventeenth-century Marranism and Jewish Apologetics*. New York: Columbia University Press, 1971.

Yovel, Yirmiyahu. "Converso Dualities In The First Generation: The Cancioneros." *Jewish Social Studies: History, Culture, and Society* 4, no. 3 (1998): 1-28.

Zeitlin, S. "Mumar and Meshumad." *The Jewish Quarterly Review* 54, no. 1 (1963): 84-86.

Zeldes, Nadia. "Legal Status of Jewish Converts to Christianity in Southern Italy and Provence." *California Italian Studies*, 1, no. 1 (2010). Accessed June 2, 2015. http://escholarship.org/uc/item/91z342hv.

Zohar, Zvi. "The Sephardic Tradition-Creative Responses to Modernity." Lecture, January 1, 2010.

Zsom, Dora. "Uncircumcised Converts in Sephardi Responsa from the Fifteenth and Sixteenth Centuries." *Iberoamerica Global* 1, no. 3 (2008): 159-71.

Zsom, Dora. "The Return of the Conversos to Judaism in the Ottoman Empire and North-Africa." *Hispania Judaica* 7 (2010): 335-47.

Zsom, Dora. "Converts in the Responsa of R. David Ibn Avi Zimra: An Analysis of the Texts." *Hispania Judaica* 6 (2008): 267-92.

Zsom, Dora. "The Levirate Marriage of Converts in the Responsa of Some Sephardic Authorities." *Kut* 3 (2008): 96-113.
De Covarrubias Horozco, Sebastian. "Tesoro De La Lengua Castellana O Española." Universidad De Sevilla-Fondo Antiguo. Accessed June 2, 2015. http://fondosdigitales.us.es/fondos/libros/765/1119/tesoro-de-la-lengua-castellana-o-espanola/.
De Salazar Acha, Jaime. "La Limpieza De Sangre." *Revista De La Inquisicion* 1 (1991): 289-308.
De Spinoza, Benedict, and R.H.M Elwes. *A Theologico-Political Treatise*. New York: Dover, 1951.
DeSola Cardoza, Anne. "Texas Mexican Secret Spanish Jews Today." Sefarad. Accessed June 9, 2015. http://sefarad.org/lm/011/texas.html.
Ldez, Andre, and Manuel Moreno. *Memorias Del Reinado De Los Reyes Católicos,*. Madrid: [Real Academia De La Historia], 1962.

Index

Abdul Hamid Siddiqui, 40, 41
Abraham, 3, 5, 13, 14, 65, 72, 73, 86, 87, 88, 90
Abraham Miguel Cardozo, 86
Almohades, 41, 49, 54, 56
Anacletus, 27
Averroës, 37
Averroism, 36, 60
Bernard of Clairvaux, 62
Christianity, 87, 91, 92
Christians, 89, 91
Ciudad Real, 83
Cologne, 11, 18
Conversos, i, 27, 31, 35, 37, 43, 57, 58, 61, 62, 63, 68, 69, 70, 71, 72, 74, 75, 76, 78, 79, 80, 82, 83, 84, 85, 86, 88, 89, 90, 91, 93
El Alboraique, 87
Elchanan, 27, 28
Fiscus Judaicus, 9
Gesta Trevorum, 16
Inquisition, 82, 83, 87, 88, 89, 90, 92
Isaac Abravanel, 83
Isaac Arama, 35
Islam, 82, 88
Jews, 82, 83, 84, 85, 86, 87, 88, 89, 90, 91, 92, 93
Joel ibn Shuaib, 35, 37
Judaism, 62, 82, 84, 85, 87, 88, 89, 91, 92, 93
Maimonides, i, 37, 38, 41, 49, 50, 51, 52, 53, 54, 55, 56, 57, 58, 61, 62, 64, 65, 67, 70, 72, 75, 84, 88

Mainz, 11, 16, 18, 21, 27, 28
Majorca, 89
Marranos, 83, 88, 89, 90, 91, 92
Moriscos, 43, 45, 46, 47, 86
Moses De Leon, 67
New Christians, 87, 88, 91
Portugal, 82, 88, 90
Rabbi Al-Fakhkhar, 65
Rabbi Asher Ben Yehiel, 66
Rabbi Eliezer, 11, 51, 52
Rabbi Ishmael, 11
Rabbi Israel de Toledo, 66
Rabbi Jonah, 64, 65
Rabbi Judah ha-Levi, 69
Rabbi Moses ben Nachman, 67
Rabbi Simon, 25, 27
Rabbi Solomon Ben Aderet, 65, 66, 73
Rabbi Solomon of Montpelier, 65
Rabbi Yochanan, 53
Rabbi Yom Tov Ishbili, 31
Rhineland, i, 7, 8, 12, 15, 21
Sefer Hasidim, 12, 13, 14
Sentencia-Estatuto, 83
Seville, 82
Shem Tov ben Shem Tov, 35, 67
Solomon Alami, 32, 35
Talmud, 82
Taqiyya, i, 37, 38, 40, 41, 42, 43, 47, 82
Toledo, 83
Valencia, 89
Visigoths, 90
Wevelinghofen, 20
Worms, 11, 16, 17, 18
Zohar, 92

ABOUT THE AUTHOR

Juan Marcos Bejarano Gutierrez is a graduate of the University of Texas at Dallas. He earned a bachelor of science in electrical engineering. He works full time as an engineer but has devoted much of his time to Jewish studies. He studied at the Siegal College of Judaic Studies in Cleveland. He received a Master of Arts Degree in Judaic Studies. He completed his doctoral studies at the Spertus Institute in Chicago in 2015. He studied at the American Seminary for Contemporary Judaism and received rabbinic ordination in 2011 from Yeshiva Mesilat Yesharim.

Juan Marcos Bejarano Gutierrez was a board member of the Society for Crypto-Judaic Studies from 2011-2013. He has published various articles in HaLapid, The Journal for Spanish, Portuguese, and Italian Crypto-Jews, and Apuntes-Theological Reflections from a Hispanic-Latino Context, and is the author of *What is Kosher?* and *What is Jewish Prayer?* and *Secret Jews: The Complex Identity of Crypto-Jews and Crypto-Judaism*. He is currently the director of the B'nai Anusim Center for Education at CryptoJewishEducation.com, which provides additional information on the Inquisition and the phenomena of Crypto-Judaism.

If you have enjoyed this book or others that are part of this series, please consider leaving a positive review on Amazon or Goodreads. A positive review helps spread the word about this book and encourages others to study and learn something new.

Made in the USA
Middletown, DE
02 January 2025

68692700R00066